CW01020704

Conversations From Calais

Photographic contributions by:
Teo Della Torre, BUILDHOLLYWOOD,
Mathilda Della Torre and Tom Weatherhilt.

Published in 2023 by Welbeck Balance
Part of Welbeck Publishing Group
Offices in: London – 20 Mortimer Street, London W1T 3JW &
Sydney – 205 Commonwealth Street, Surry Hills 2010
www.welbeckpublishing.com

Text, design and layout © Welbeck Non-Fiction Ltd 2023
Introduction text © Mathilda Della Torre 2023

All rights reserved. No part of this publication may be reproduced, stored in a retrieval system, or transmitted in any form or by any means,electronically, mechanical, photocopying, recording or otherwise, without the prior permission of the copyright owners and the publishers.

A CIP catalogue record for this book is available from the British Library.

ISBN
Hardback – 978-1-80129-245-0

Typeset by stevewilliamscreative.com
Printed in the UK by Bell & Bain Ltd

10 9 8 7 6 5 4 3 2 1

Note/Disclaimer

Welbeck Balance encourages diversity and different viewpoints. However, all views, thoughts, and opinions expressed in this book are the author's own and are not necessarily representative of Welbeck Publishing Group as an organization. All material in this book is set out in good faith for general guidance; Welbeck Publishing Group makes no representations or warranties of any kind, express or implied, with respect to the accuracy, completeness, suitability or currency of the contents of this book, and specifically disclaims, to the extent permitted by law, any implied warranties of merchantability or fitness for a particular purpose and any injury, illness, damage, death, liability or loss incurred, directly or indirectly from the use or application of any of the information contained in this book.

ABOUT CONVERSATIONS FROM CALAIS

Founded in 2018, Conversations From Calais is a global art movement that captures conversations between volunteers and refugees in poster form. Pasted on our city walls, these posters amplify voices in human moments and bear witness to those who are often ignored.

MATHILDA DELLA TORRE's work focuses on co-designing projects with local communities. She is interested in creating ways to transition to a sustainable and just society using the power of design. She is the founder of Conversations From Calais, and is currently working as a community manager at PIE Factory, home of the positive impact experience, developing brand activations and community projects that help shape a better world.

@conversationsfromcalais

CONTENTS

INTRODUCTION

Refugees on dinghies crossing the Channel. The ongoing crisis. Asylum seekers "invading" our coastlines.

I had read the headlines, seen the photos and heard the politicians – but somehow it didn't hit home the way it should have. It felt too big and overwhelming to tackle, something I could put to the back of my mind and ignore for a little while longer.

I remember reading an article about the so-called Calais Jungle and thinking that couldn't possibly be true, not in Europe, not in France, not so close to home. It was hard to fathom, but it stayed, lingering in the back of my mind. I talked to friends and family, and I sought out more information, but it was difficult to truly understand what was happening. Slowly, I felt more and more guilty about being born on this side of the world, with a passport that allowed me to go anywhere I wanted. The guilt stayed with me; I needed to act in some way.

It was my mother who suggested we go to Calais to help in a small way. And so, in September 2018, we spent ten days in Northern France, unpacking and sorting bags of donations in a volunteer warehouse and then distributing them in temporary camps around Calais and Dunkirk, where displaced communities live. Together with other volunteers, we were trying in the best way we could to make these unbearable realities a little more bearable. To this day, I have never felt so hopeless and so hopeful at the same time. Being surrounded by people who had decided to stand up against governments that had denied them simple human rights was so humbling and powerful; at the same time, I could see that the aid we were providing was a mere drop in the ocean.

Many of the voiceless are talking all the time. They are loud when we get close enough to hear them and if we are capable of truly listening.

Each time I returned to Calais, I witnessed so much misery and pain; but when people asked me about my visits, I found myself remembering the small details of life. I talked about the taste of the curry and rice I handed out, a drawing of a flower on a piece of paper, the red hoodie that no one wanted, the hellos and goodbyes in French, English, Italian, Farsi, Tigrinya and Arabic. I told them about someone from Afghanistan who had been travelling for five years. He'd worked as an engineer, a teacher, a mechanic and a waiter while on his journey. When he reached Calais, he was so tired he didn't even have the energy to try and cross to the UK at night, so he would walk up a hill and look over the Channel to see if he could spot the British coastline. He told me to look for him in the streets of England, which I still catch myself doing. I told them about a young man who had left his family in Eritrea and who loved to speak in broken Italian with me. He was a healthcare assistant back home and all he wanted was to get to the UK, work in a hospital and bring his kids here, so they could grow up somewhere they felt safe and valued. I will never forget the day my phone lit up with a Facebook message from him saying, “Hi, I am in the UK, two days ago”.

These stories stayed with me, and my impulse to share them with the world grew. I wanted people to see *this* side of Calais. I began the process of trying to figure out how I could use my design skills to share what volunteers were witnessing. But how could I authentically portray a situation that I had only had a glimpse of? How could I talk about displacement when my passport gave me easy access to almost anywhere in the world?

I went back to the purest form of sharing, storytelling. I simplified the stories I had heard from the people I’d met into short conversations. I structured these as first-person accounts from the perspective of the volunteer recalling conversations with an anonymous migrant. I wanted to find a way to share these conversations with a wider audience. I turned to wheat pasting – this involves pasting up posters using a glue made from flour and water; the natural glue allows you to post in public spaces without having to ask for permission. This direct action technique is a simple, visual means for communicating – and it’s quick, easy, cheap and effective. I knew I could easily make the glue, print the posters and cover the streets with them. So in October 2019, I took the train from London to Dover and pasted up my first set of posters using the glue I had made that morning.

This is how *Conversations From Calais* came to life. I've been pasting up conversations and sharing them on social media ever since. The project seeks to re-humanize those affected by the refugee crisis by using public space to share conversations volunteers have had with migrants in Calais over the years. It's a way of bearing witness to the thousands of displaced people trying to reach the UK, whose voices are so often silenced or ignored.

By pasting these posters on walls around the world, we take over public space and refuse to let the refugee narrative be dominated by mainstream media and politicians.

This ever-growing collection focuses on capturing the diversity of experiences, and tries to resist creating new stereotypes of refugees as villains, heroic figures or hopeless victims. By pasting these posters on walls around the world, we take over public space and refuse to let the refugee narrative be dominated by mainstream media and politicians who use the same scapegoating strategies they've been using for years.

This book is a continuation of this project, but it is also a way of creating a space to hear from people who have used their voices to defend refugee rights. People who have often been silenced. I asked eight contributors to respond to a selection of themes that these conversations cover. They wrote about what it feels like to be the daughter of Palestinian refugees, about the lifelong journey to integration in the UK, about the pain and joy that comes with remembering a traumatic past.

I hope this multi-voiced account which includes different perspectives of the displaced experience is used as a starting point to delve deeper into the topic. These conversations were had in Calais, but they are happening all around the world, whether that is on the US–Mexico border, on the Greek islands or in Turkey.

Many of the voiceless are talking all the time. They are loud when we get close enough to hear them and if we are capable of truly listening. We've not been listening to migrant and displaced communities for a long time, but they've always been there. This book is my way of documenting the oral history of conversations in Calais in the hope of immortalising these voices. It is also my hope that it will encourage more of us to listen.

mathildadellatorre.

It's important that we remember that these conversations only represent a step in a long journey. For displaced communities in Calais, reaching the UK is usually the ultimate goal, but obtaining a safe and warm welcome is rarely the case. I have chosen Freedom From Torture as our charity partner. Each book sold supports their mission and their work to raise awareness and campaign for survivors' rights in the UK.

"These are vital conversations. Everyone should eavesdrop on them."

KAMILA SHAMSIE, Author of award-winning bestseller *Home Fire*

01

HOME &
ELONGING

You asked me if the world knew this was happening, if the world knew you were here, if the world knew your tent was taken from you almost every night, if the world knew the police was spraying tear gas on you almost every day, if the world knew this was living hell. And all I could do was whisper yes, yes the world knows.

@conversationsfromcalais

You want
football s
the grass
teams. As
team won
unfair bec
too good a
with the ba
was unfair
run away a
world and
stop me.

You didn't want a green or purple sweater, you wanted a black one. We didn't have any black ones left so I offered you a dark blue one. You looked at me and asked if one day you'd have a choice again. I told you I really hoped so and handed you the dark blue sweater.

You were helping me pick up the trash around the camp, when you saw the police drive by and said the police was no good. I replied that you were right, that the police was not protecting you, that the police was no good. You were only nine years old.

n the
re
owers
a rose
si, so
say
ch. You
asier
ou
helped
u said
ite
had

@conversationsf

You asked me how I was doing and I said I didn't want to go back to the UK tomorrow but that I had to. You laughed at me and said that we lived in a strange world, because reaching the UK was all you had ever wanted.

You wanted
toothbrush a
to cross the
you the toot
apologised a
having a boa
your bag was
legs tired and
cold. I gave y
tea and apolo
the cold. You
and walked a

onversationsfromcalais

ESSAY BY

OSMAN YOUSEFZADA

MULTI-DISCIPLINARY ARTIST,
WRITER & SOCIAL ACTIVIST

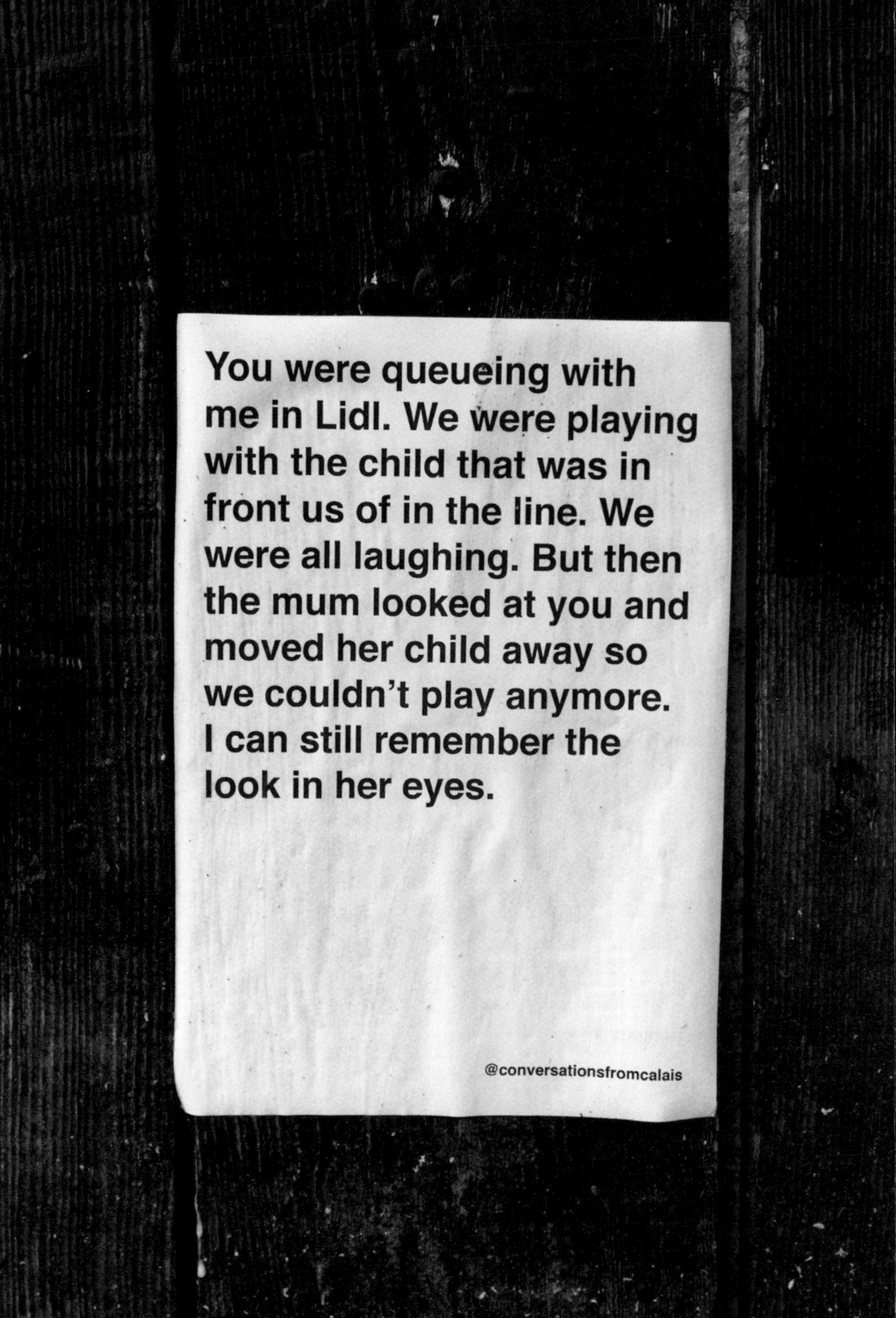

You were queueing with me in Lidl. We were playing with the child that was in front us of in the line. We were all laughing. But then the mum looked at you and moved her child away so we couldn't play anymore. I can still remember the look in her eyes.

@conversationsfromcalais

WHERE ARE YOU REALLY FROM?

Where are you really from?
But where are you *really* from?

Intermittently, this query hunts me down. The same question that sends my atoms into a spin, disrupting my inner compass, its magnetic force unable to fathom which direction to point. East or West? Where do I belong? I protest that I am from here. It is a question so casual, sometimes friendly, yet often guised with under-currents of race, class and nationalism. As if the inquisitor is also the warden, mentally totting up how many have been let in. The colour of my skin and my ebony hair and beard give me away. There is too much melanin for fortress Europe; this melanin is more in obedience with the tropic of Cancer, where it glistens in its overhead sun. So, where am I really from?

I've made myself a home in London, but the question still keeps coming: where am I really from?

I was born inside the womb of Queen Elizabeth – the hospital. Bang in the centre of England – in Birmingham, a city that terrifies the neo-nationalists with its wrong sort of immigrants. The tabloids and broadsheets alike rebrand it as the jihadi capital of England. A minority majority city in the making, England's second city will become non-white soon. In that Regina-christened maternity ward, a young immigrant lady from the borders of Pakistan and Afghanistan will give birth to her four British children. Mum had travelled across seas, in a white shuttlecock burqa – an embroidered hat on her head, which gathered fabric that cascaded over her modesty. Her husband already here, doing the factory jobs that no one wanted; the fires of the foundries burned, the hot crucibles poured, and dad and his friends were the immigrant alchemists making Britain great again.

East or West? Where do I belong? I protest that I am from here.

They eventually swapped their green passports for black British ones, then came the red European ones and now we have the dark blue Brexit ones. This machine-readable document, with our biometrics embedded in code, is the passport that allows me to traverse the world like a master, with few visa restrictions, while my cousins in Pakistan attempt to roam the world like slaves. Working on construction sites in the Middle East, sometimes these booklets of nationhood and belonging are seized to avoid them fleeing from the hard grind and bitter midday sun.

I come from a generation of carpenters, who craft with materials like wood, maple, mahogany, oak, brick, clay, straw – it is in my blood. We are builders and makers of homes. I've made myself a home in London, but the question still keeps coming: where am I really from? I had my DNA tested recently and, occasionally, cousins pop into my inbox; stretching from

You looked at me and said you were not illegal and that you were not coming to the UK for £37 a week. You said you didn't want anything more than a safe life.
@conversationsfromcalais

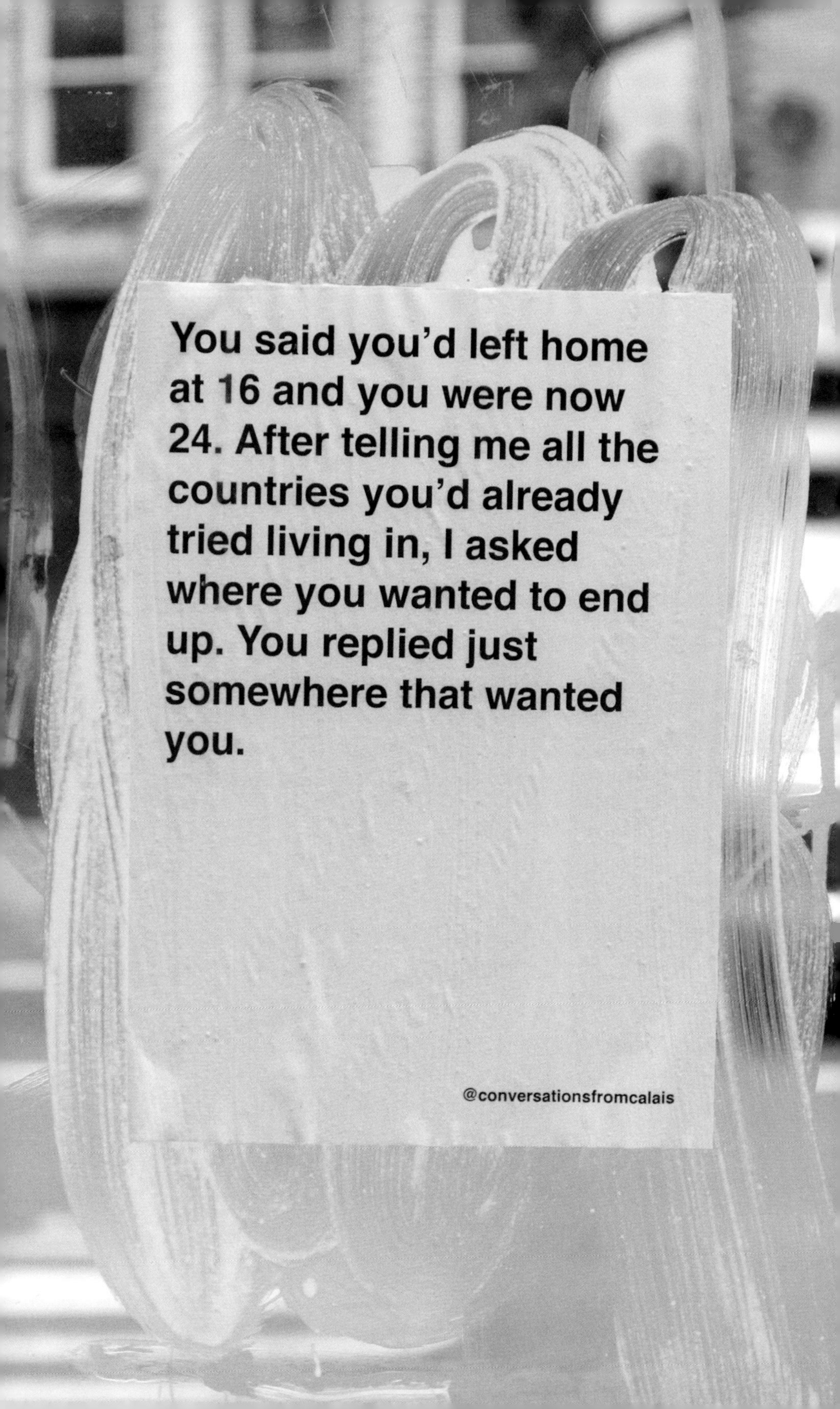

You said you'd left home at 16 and you were now 24. After telling me all the countries you'd already tried living in, I asked where you wanted to end up. You replied just somewhere that wanted you.

@conversationsfromcalais

Badakhshan and Kabul in Afghanistan, to Attock and Lahore in Pakistan, and across the partition lines into India, where they have Hindu and Sikh names. There they circle holy fires and holy books, while we aim to circle Mecca in white.

Where am I really from?

This DNA test has unlocked cousins in Malaysia, in Iran, in East Africa. Then there are my white cousins from Ireland, with names like Kennedy, who live in America. I share over 10 per cent of my DNA with them – was it colonial rape, or inter-racial love? One of my great-great-great-great grandparents took a child from the empire and raised it, passing them off as white. Does that get me a Green Card? Shall I ask them, just as my near cousins in Pakistan ask me routinely to facilitate a safe passage to England. I can't begrudge anyone wanting a better life.

I have the official papers; I was born with them – an automatic right to the first world. But do let me know where I'm really from.

OSMAN YOUSEFZADA is a British-born multi-disciplinary artist. His practice revolves around modes of storytelling, merging autobiography with fiction and ritual. His work is concerned with the representation and rupture of the migrational experience and makes reference to socio-political issues of today. These themes are explored through moving image, installations, text works, sculpture, garment making and performance.

osmanstudio.com
@osmanstudio

BUILDHOLLYWOOD
You had taught yourself how to speak nine new languages from the day you left your home, so you could speak with the people of every country you crossed. I said I didn't know anyone who could speak this many languages. You replied that it was useless anyway, because no one ever wanted to speak to you, let alone look at you.
@conversationsfromcalais
BUILDHOLLYWOOD

“Refugees are just people like you and me, with the same dreams, ambitions and fears that we all share. Like all of us, refugees simply want to be part of a community they can call home and the chance to live their lives in safety. It is so important that we hear their voices and see our own hopes and fears reflected in what they say.”

LORD ALF DUBS, Labour peer & campaigner

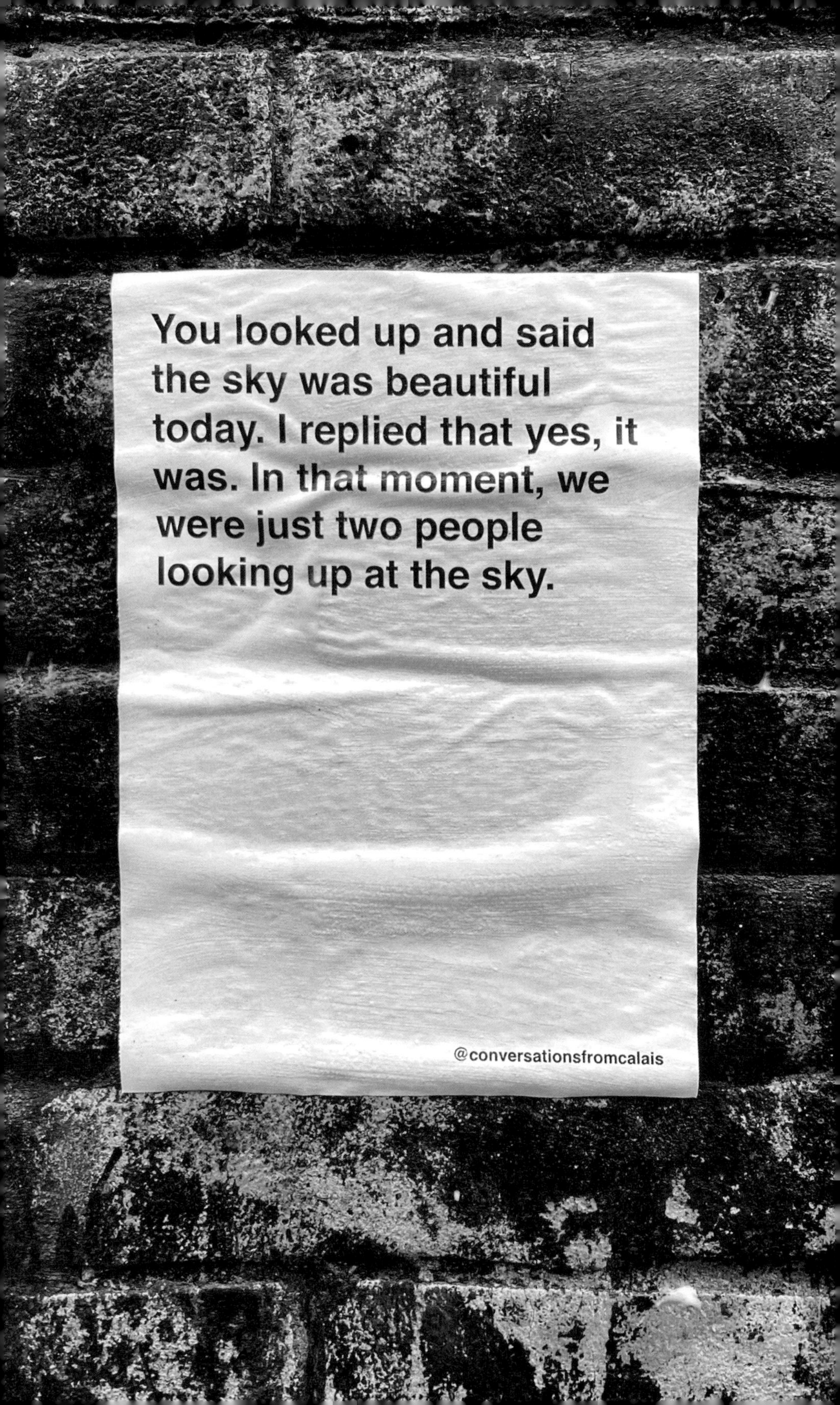
You looked up and said the sky was beautiful today. I replied that yes, it was. In that moment, we were just two people looking up at the sky.
@conversationsfromcalais

You were 18 years old, and the middle child out of 12 brothers and sisters. After charging your phone, you came back to tell me your mother had just had another child. You said tomorrow you would call her to ask if it was a boy or a girl.

@conversationsfromcalais

"I remember when I was leaving Calais someone from home said to me that it was good that I was going back into 'the real world'. I told them that I had learnt more about the real world during nine months in France than I probably ever had before."

FRANKIE, Volunteer

You showed me photos of your little boy as we handed you bags of nappies. They were the exact nappies I used for my little girl at home and I told you about her. The fact our lives were so similar and yet so different hit me like a tonne of bricks.

@conversationsfromcalais

you wanted
because
lived there.
cousin lived
told me
your
been too
killed

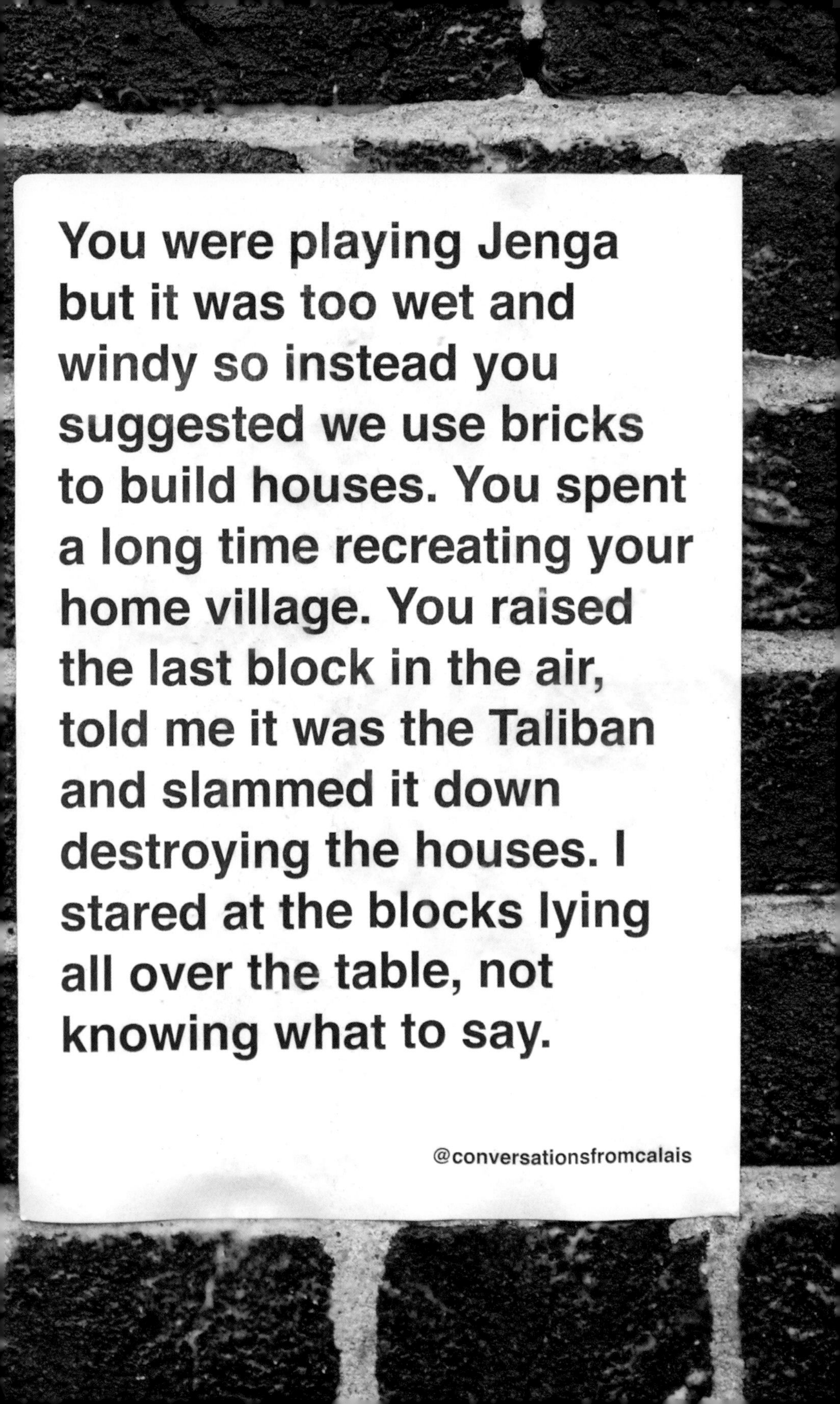

You were playing Jenga but it was too wet and windy so instead you suggested we use bricks to build houses. You spent a long time recreating your home village. You raised the last block in the air, told me it was the Taliban and slammed it down destroying the houses. I stared at the blocks lying all over the table, not knowing what to say.

@conversationsfromcalais

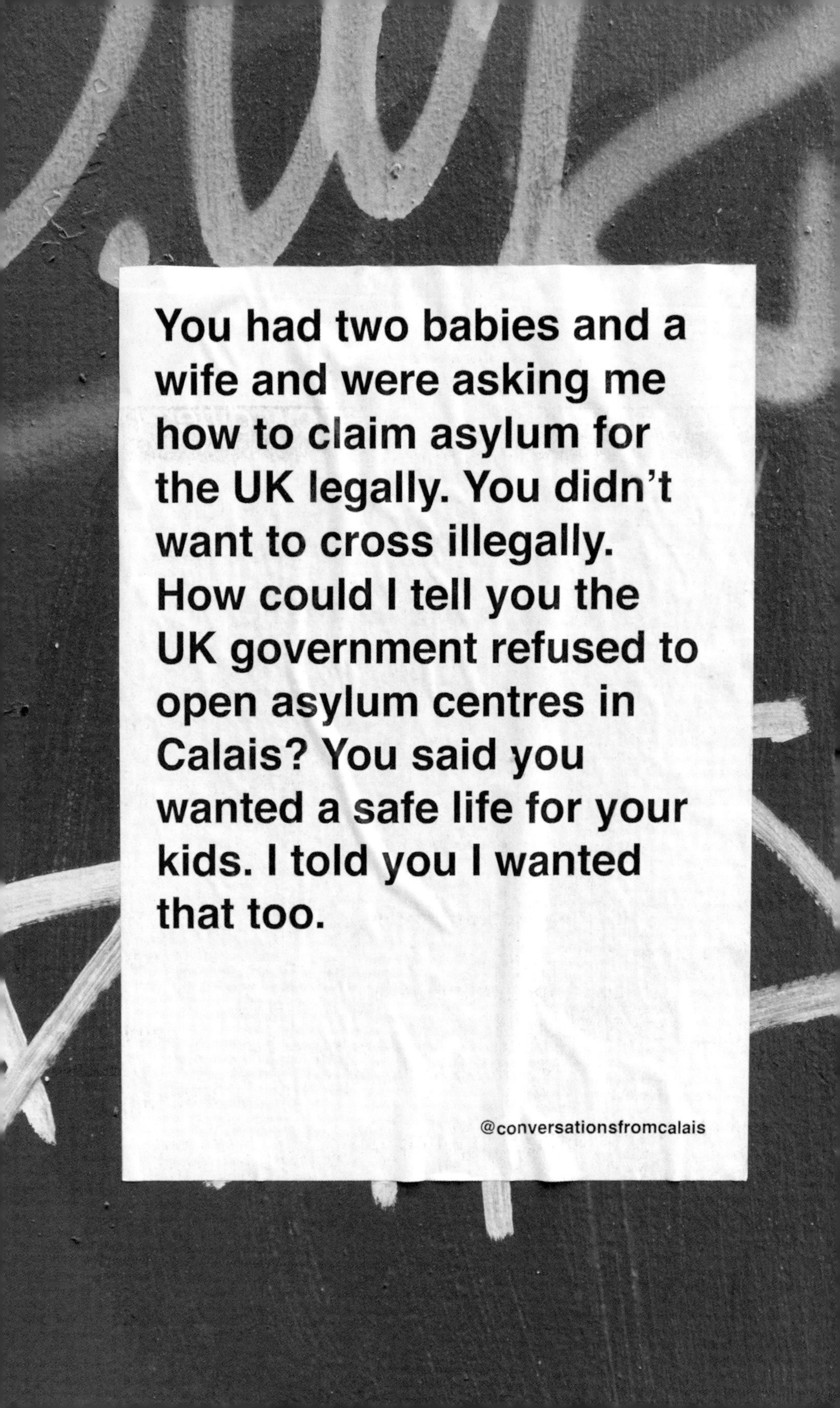

You had two babies and a wife and were asking me how to claim asylum for the UK legally. You didn't want to cross illegally. How could I tell you the UK government refused to open asylum centres in Calais? You said you wanted a safe life for your kids. I told you I wanted that too.

@conversationsfromcalais

"Difficult truths are too easy to ignore, and if a story slips down the news agenda it is convenient to believe that a resolution has been attained. It's also easy to suppose that the victims of these tragedies are somehow different from you and I – to forget that they too have families, children and careers and that they too feel love and fear. Can we really imagine ourselves in their place?"

MARK TITCHNER, Artist

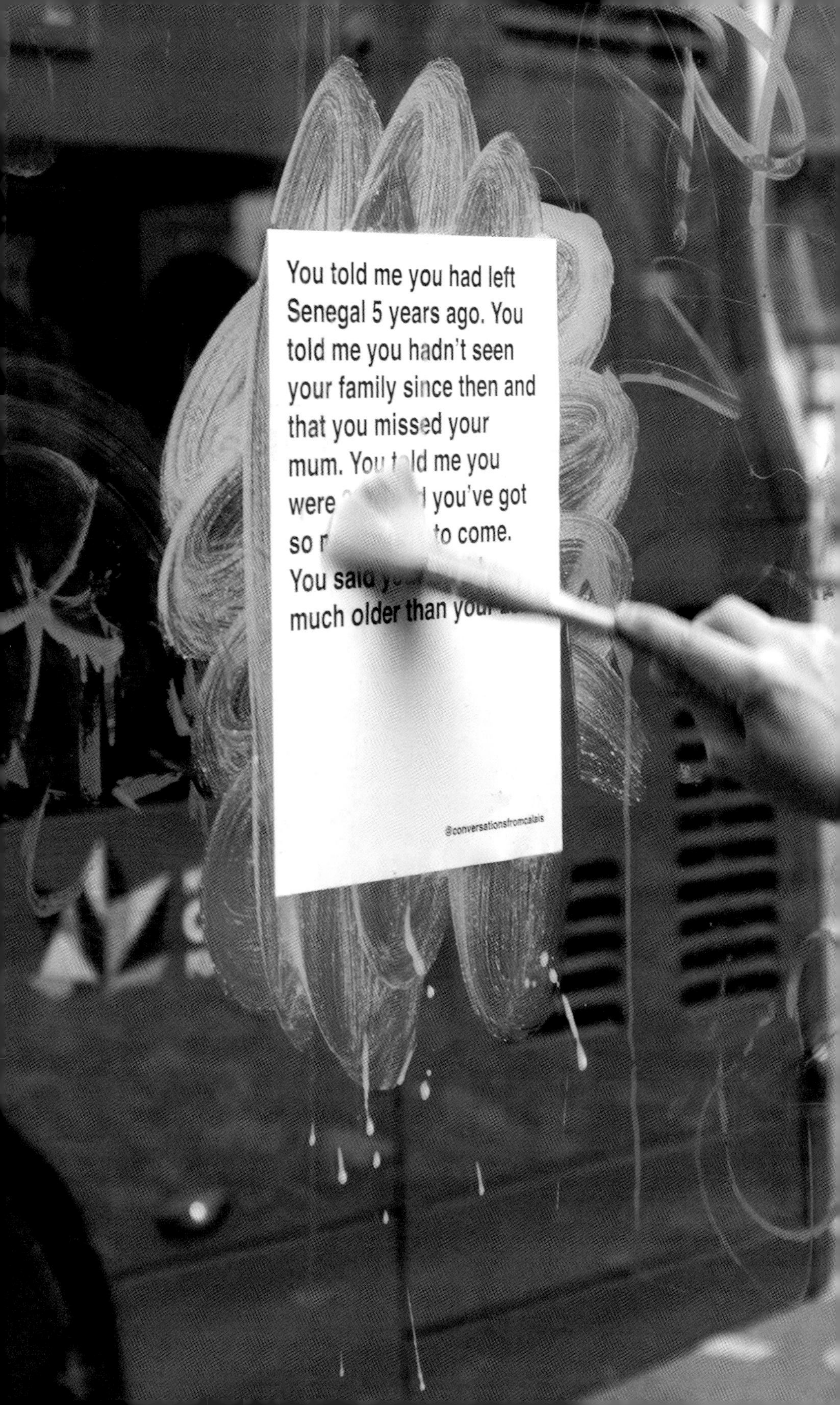
You told me you had left
Senegal 5 years ago. You
told me you hadn't seen
your family since then and
that you missed your
mum. You
me you
were
you've got
so
to come.
You said
much older than
@conversationsfromcalais

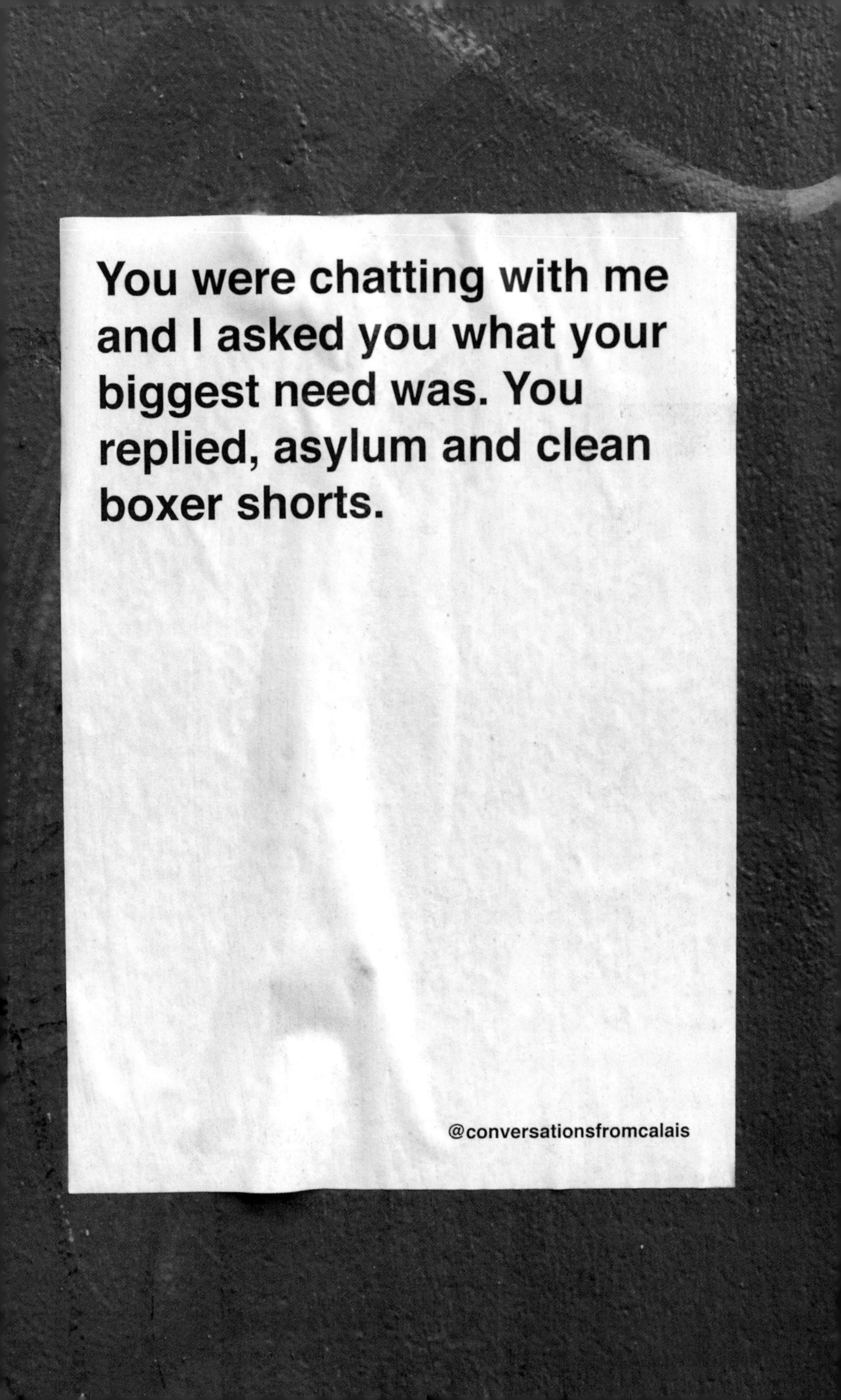

You were chatting with me and I asked you what your biggest need was. You replied, asylum and clean boxer shorts.

@conversationsfromcalais

02

JOURNEY & TRAVEL

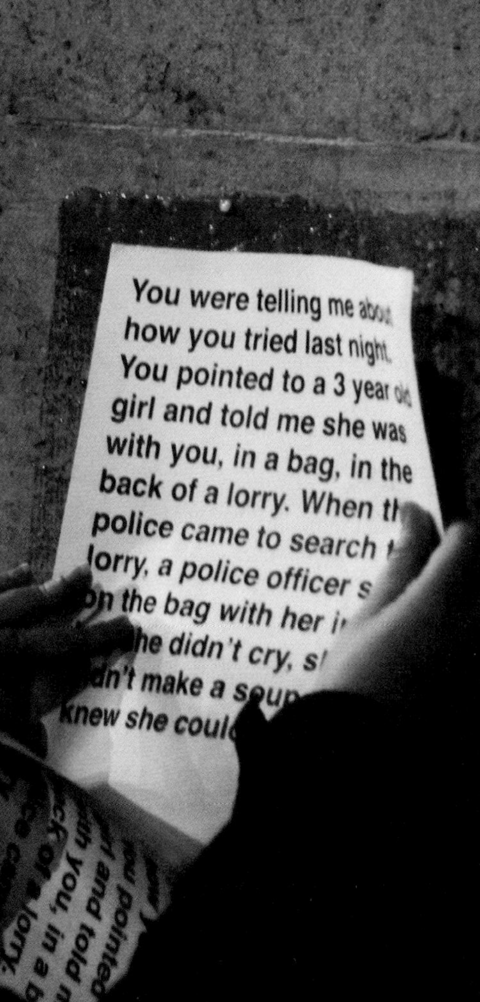
You were telling me
how you tried last night.
You pointed to a 3 year
girl and told me she was
with you, in a bag, in the
back of a lorry. When
police came to search
lorry, a police officer
the bag with her
didn't cry,
make a
knew she

ESSAY BY

GULWALI PASSARLAY

AUTHOR & ACTIVIST

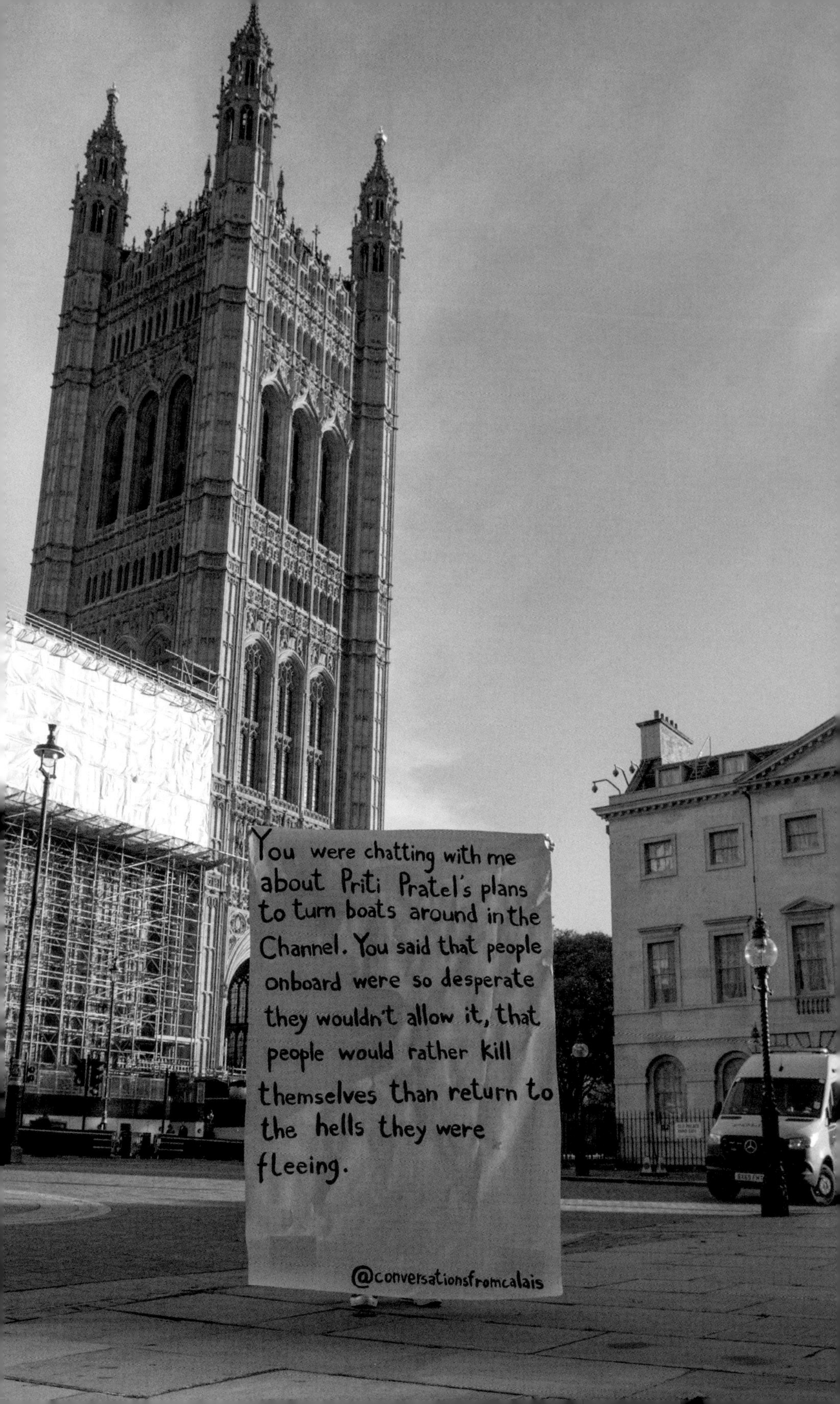
You were chatting with me about Priti Pratel's plans to turn boats around in the Channel. You said that people onboard were so desperate they wouldn't allow it, that people would rather kill themselves than return to the hells they were fleeing.
@conversationsfromcalais

A LIFELONG JOURNEY

I was still a child when my father was killed in a gun battle with the US army in Afghanistan. The Taliban told me I would have to fight or I would also die. So, when I was 12 years old, my family decided that I must flee the country. That's when my journey began.

I walked through countries including Iran, Turkey, Bulgaria, Greece, Italy and France. On the way, I was arrested, assaulted, imprisoned, deported, humiliated by authorities and treated as a commodity by smugglers. I endured a 50-hour long journey without food or drink, before getting into a lorry in Calais. I crossed 7,150 miles through 10 countries in order to reach safety 12 months later, when I made it to the UK.

For a lot of Afghan people, I am too British or too Westernized. For a lot of British people, I am too Afghan or too Muslim.

There are moments from that year I try to forget, and there are some I often think of. I remember so clearly when I tried walking through the Iranian border into Turkey for the second time. As I stood in the no-man's land between the two countries, I saw before me a very different view to the one I had seen the first time.

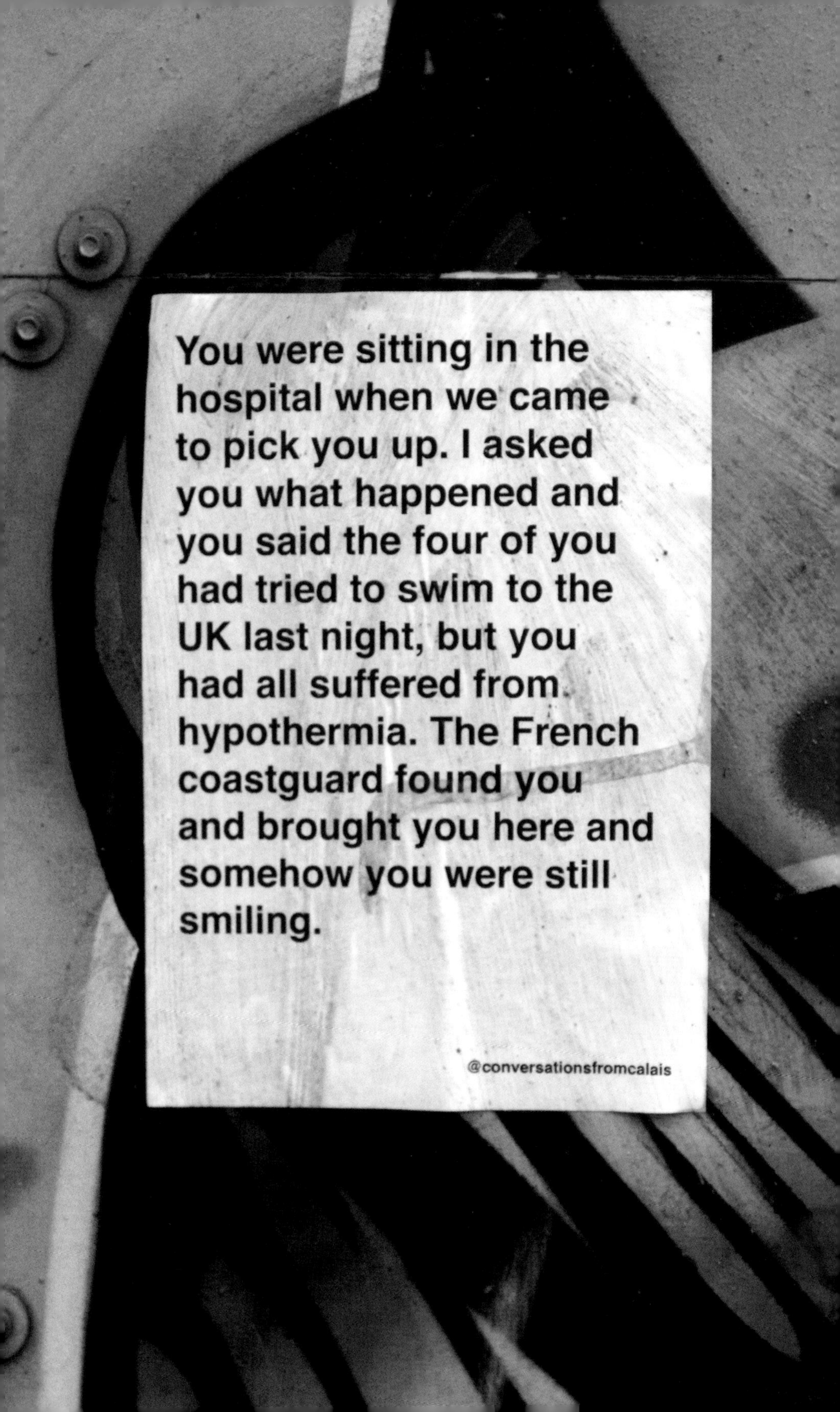

You were sitting in the hospital when we came to pick you up. I asked you what happened and you said the four of you had tried to swim to the UK last night, but you had all suffered from hypothermia. The French coastguard found you and brought you here and somehow you were still smiling.

@conversationsfromcalais

At that time, just a couple of weeks into my journey, I was still a frightened child. I had been transfixed as I had looked to one side of the horizon and seen night, and on the other side seen day. This time, the rocky landscape looked the same, and it was impossible to tell how and where Turkey differed from Iran, but I felt a new sensation. It was as though I was standing between two worlds – the old and the new. My old and my new.

I calculated it must be close to seven months since I had left my home and my family. I was still no closer to Western Europe, but I had changed. I was no longer a little boy. I might still look like one, but I certainly wasn't one inside. How could I be? I had been beaten, abused and arrested. I had known hunger, fear and misery.

I now have a home, a family and a life here in the UK, yet I continue to be labelled as a refugee, as a migrant and, for some, I will never be a citizen.

My journey is one of becoming an adult, while still living in a child's body. I hadn't thought about this while I was travelling. Back then, my priorities consisted of surviving on the little food, water and other necessities we could find. Living this way for so long, and with so many people, made it seem normal.

It took five years of waiting for my asylum claim to be approved in the UK for me to really understand how much my journey had shaped me. Physically, psychologically and emotionally, it had transformed me. It created the man and father I am today.

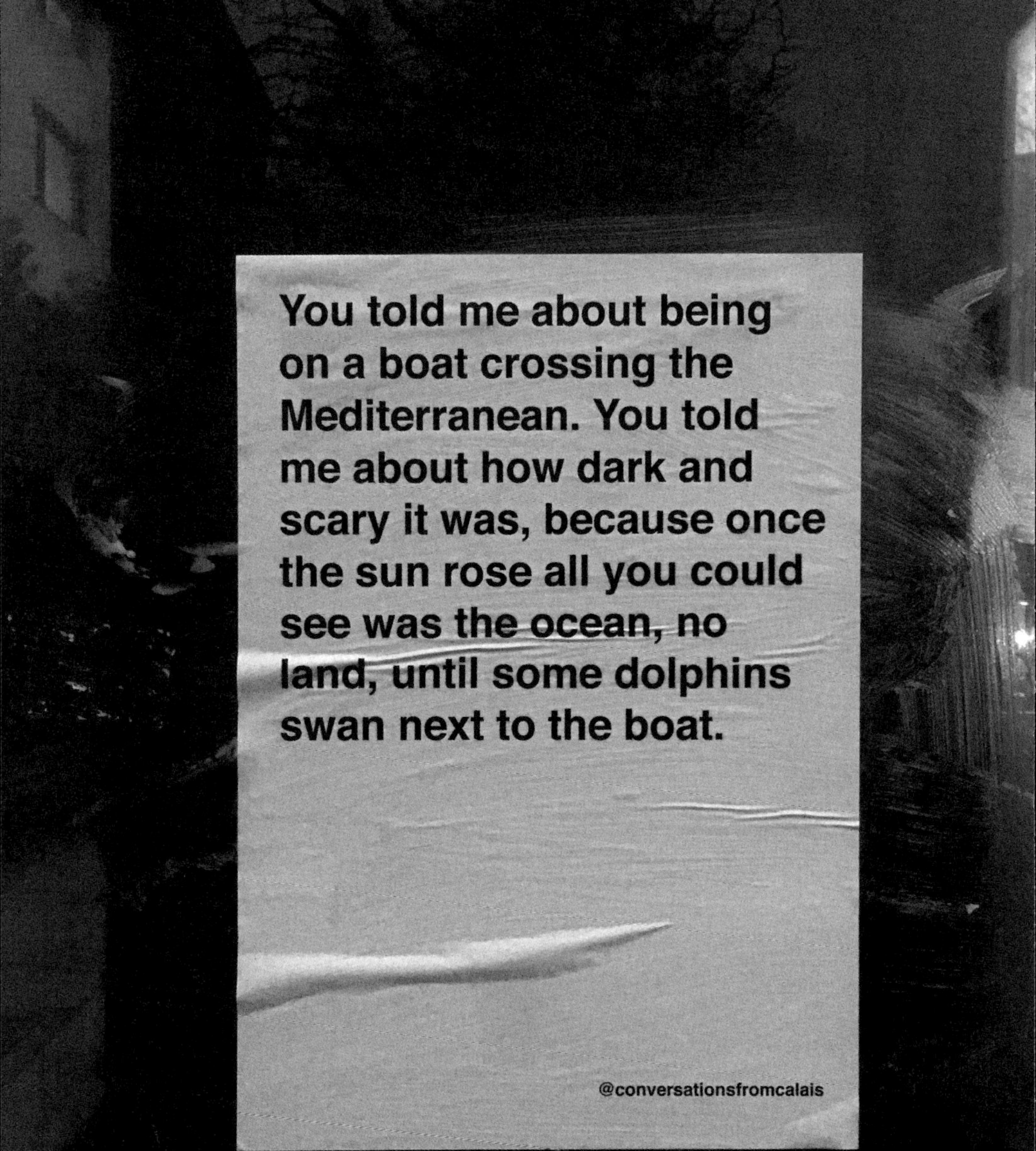

You told me about being on a boat crossing the Mediterranean. You told me about how dark and scary it was, because once the sun rose all you could see was the ocean, no land, until some dolphins swan next to the boat.

@conversationsfromcalais

That journey, as an undocumented migrant travelling to seek safety, has now ended. I became a British citizen 14 years later. I now have a home, a family and a life here in the UK, yet I continue to be labelled as a refugee, as a migrant and, for some, I will never be a citizen. For a lot of Afghan people, I am too British or too Westernized. For a lot of British people, I am too Afghan or too Muslim. The struggle for my rights, my belonging and my acceptance in this country continues. That will be a lifelong journey.

I calculated it must be close to seven months since I had left my home and my family. I was still no closer to Western Europe, but I had changed. I was no longer a little boy.

GULWALI PASSARLAY is an advocate, humanitarian and spokesperson for refugees and asylum seekers across the UK. Since arriving in the UK in 2007, after being forced to leave Afghanistan as a 12-year-old boy, he has been a political campaigner for refugees' rights, social justice and education. The experience of his journey to the UK shaped his future and inspired an insatiable determination and commitment to raise awareness and make a difference for other refugees. In 2015, he published his autobiography *The Lightless Sky: My Journey to Safety as a Child Refugee*. Some of this essay is from that book.

gulwalipassarlay.wordpress.com
@gulwali_passarlay
@GulwaliP

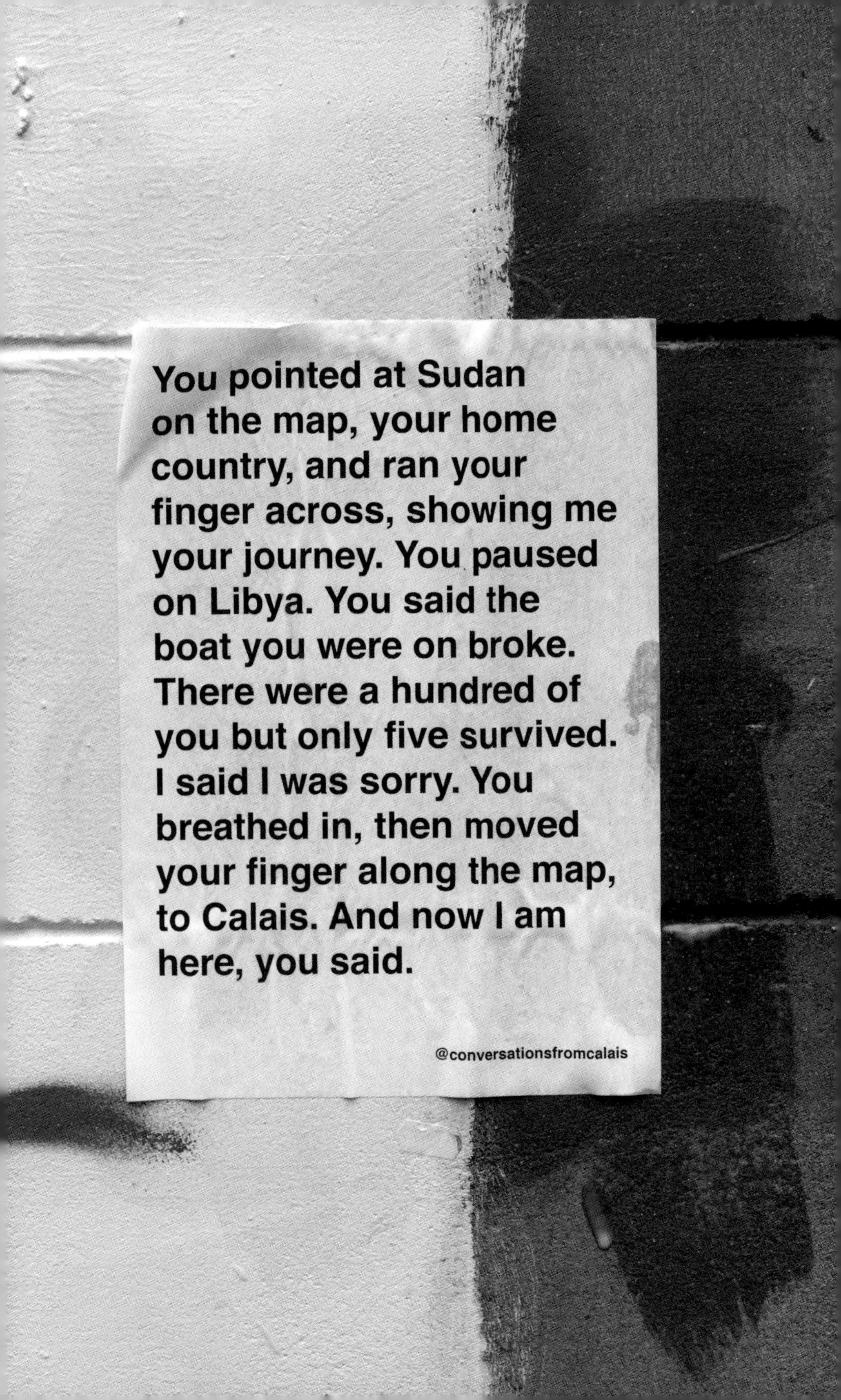

You pointed at Sudan on the map, your home country, and ran your finger across, showing me your journey. You paused on Libya. You said the boat you were on broke. There were a hundred of you but only five survived. I said I was sorry. You breathed in, then moved your finger along the map, to Calais. And now I am here, you said.

@conversationsfromcalais

You asked me for a plastic bag and I thought you were a volunteer because of your thick London accent. You told me you had lived in the UK since you were three, but a year ago you were charged with a minor offence and you were deported to Afghanistan, a country you couldn't remember. As soon as you arrived in Kabul, you turned around and began your journey back home, as a refugee.

@conversationsfromcalais

You were still here. It had been 3 months since I'd last volunteered in Calais, and yet we were still having the same conversation. You said that you'd been trying to cross every day since we last saw each other.

You told me that back in Greece, you used to swim in the sea, in the evening. It was your meditation. Your way of getting away from the camp. You said we all needed to learn to swim, or else we would drown.

@conversationsfromcalais

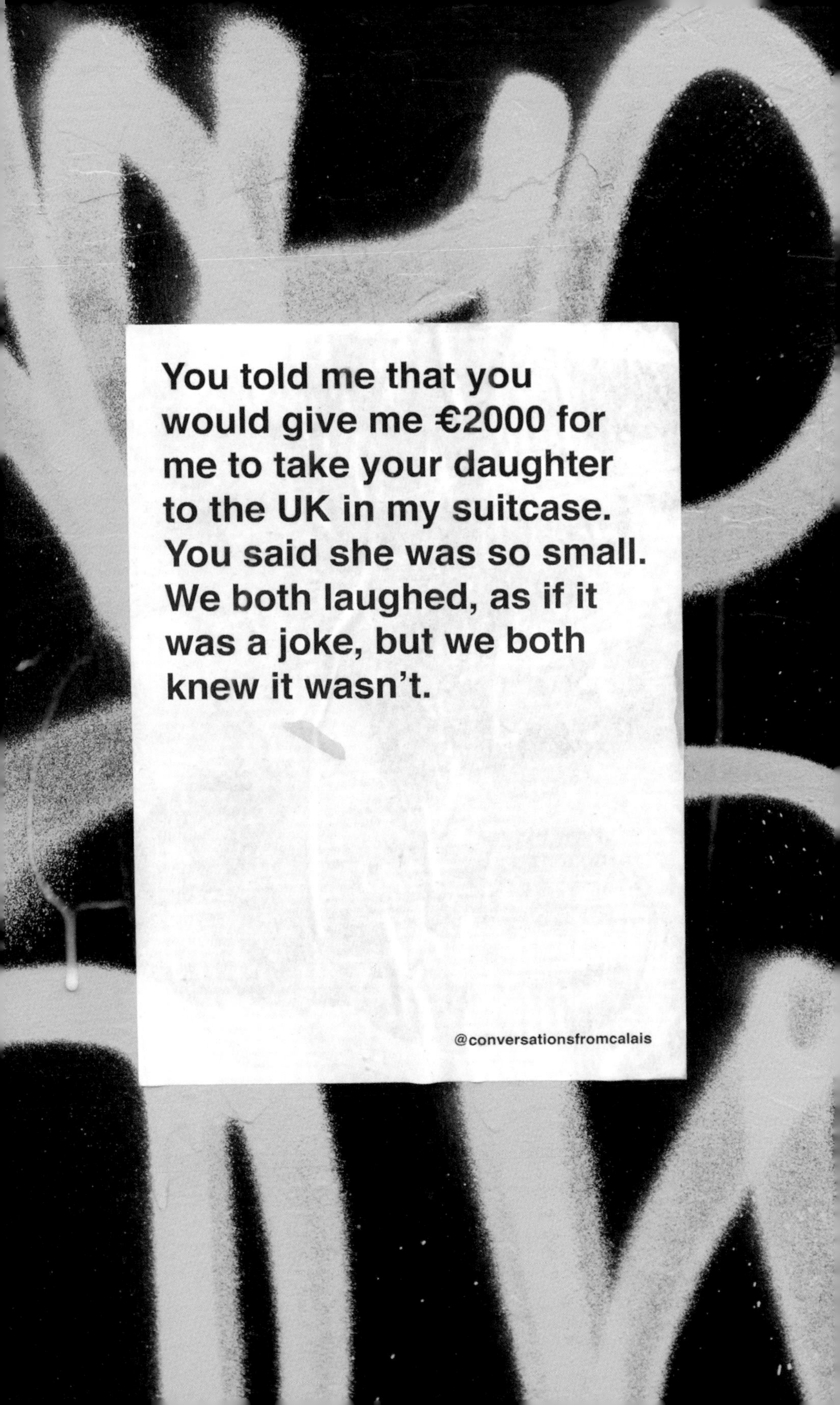
You told me that you would give me €2000 for me to take your daughter to the UK in my suitcase. You said she was so small. We both laughed, as if it was a joke, but we both knew it wasn't.
@conversationsfromcalais

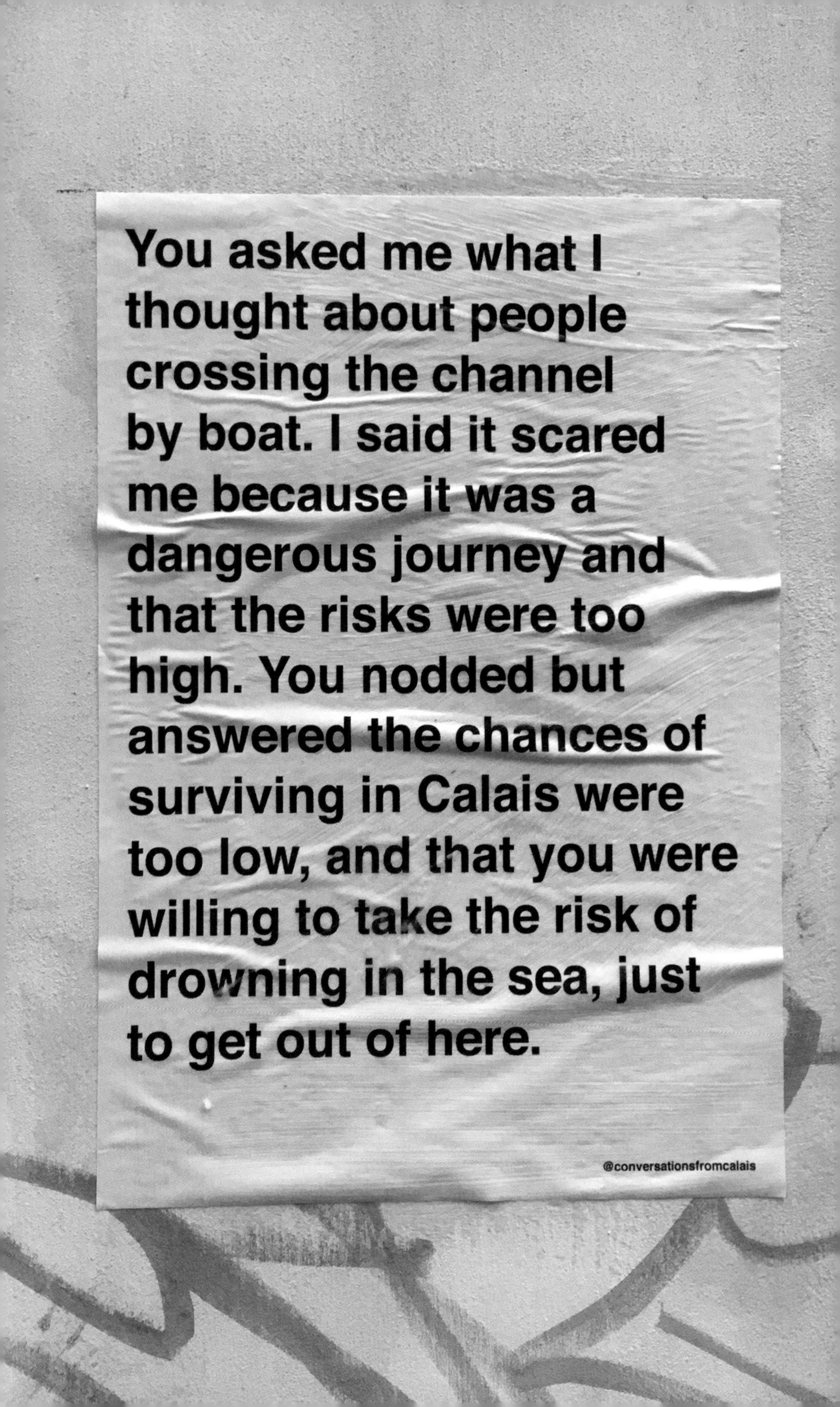

You asked me what I thought about people crossing the channel by boat. I said it scared me because it was a dangerous journey and that the risks were too high. You nodded but answered the chances of surviving in Calais were too low, and that you were willing to take the risk of drowning in the sea, just to get out of here.

@conversationsfromcalais

“Volunteering in Calais for 4 months provided some of the hardest and some of the best days of my life. One man once said to me, ‘We could survive without having volunteers here’, and another replied, ‘Yes, we could, but it makes getting up in the morning easier knowing there are people here who care if we live or die.’”

BETH, Volunteer

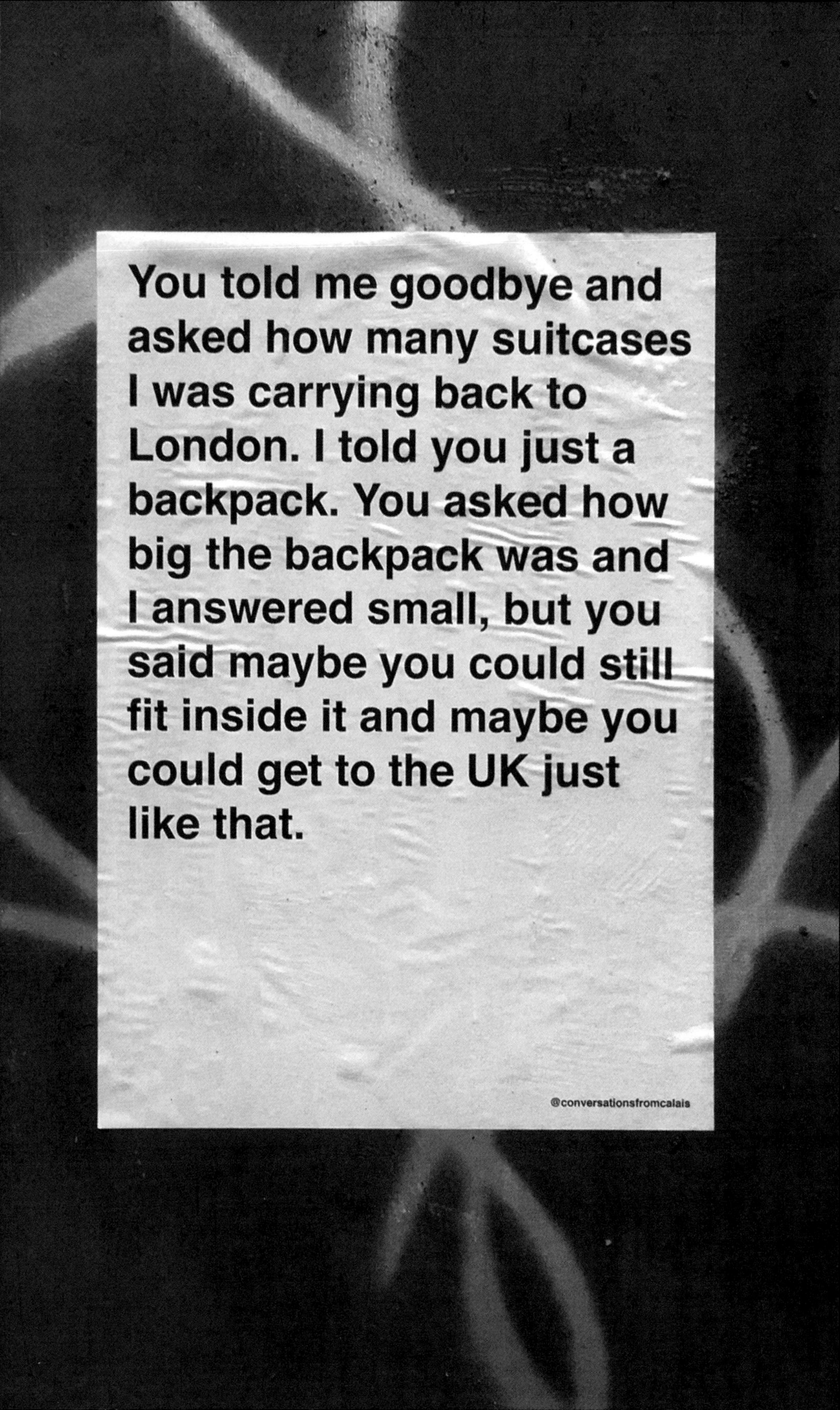

You told me goodbye and asked how many suitcases I was carrying back to London. I told you just a backpack. You asked how big the backpack was and I answered small, but you said maybe you could still fit inside it and maybe you could get to the UK just like that.

@conversationsfromcalais

ust.
Dont

You were sitting in the
hospital when we came
to pick
up. I asked
you
appened and
you
he four of you
had
to swim to the
UK
ight, but you
ha
uffered from
hy
rmia. The French
co
uard found you
an
rought you here and
so
you were still

@conversationsfromcalais

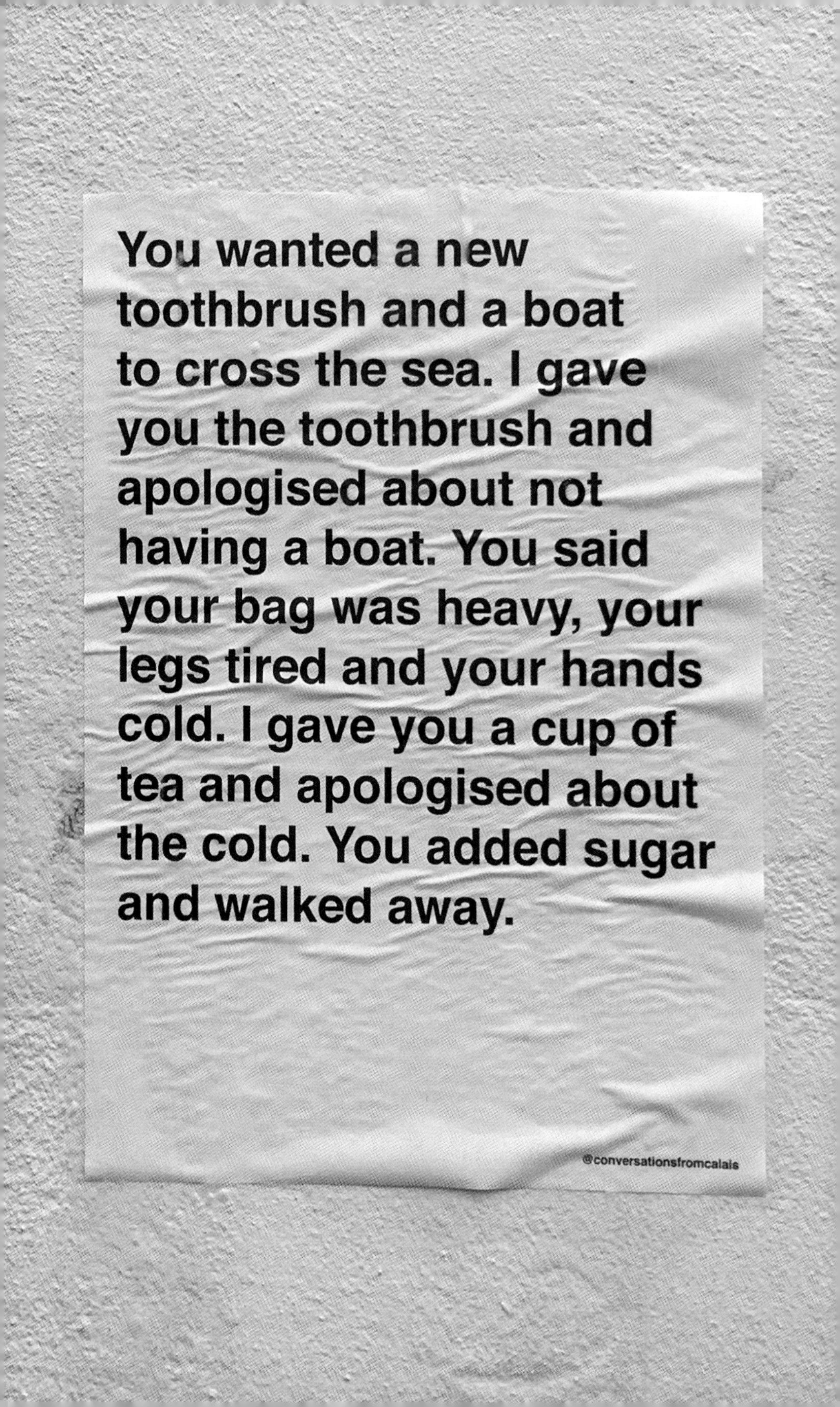

You wanted a new toothbrush and a boat to cross the sea. I gave you the toothbrush and apologised about not having a boat. You said your bag was heavy, your legs tired and your hands cold. I gave you a cup of tea and apologised about the cold. You added sugar and walked away.

@conversationsfromcalais

“These conversations are history in the making. Just a few lines on an A4 piece of paper can evoke emotion in all of us.”

JAZ O’HARA, Human rights activist & founder of The Worldwide Tribe

03

KINDNESS &
ONNECTION

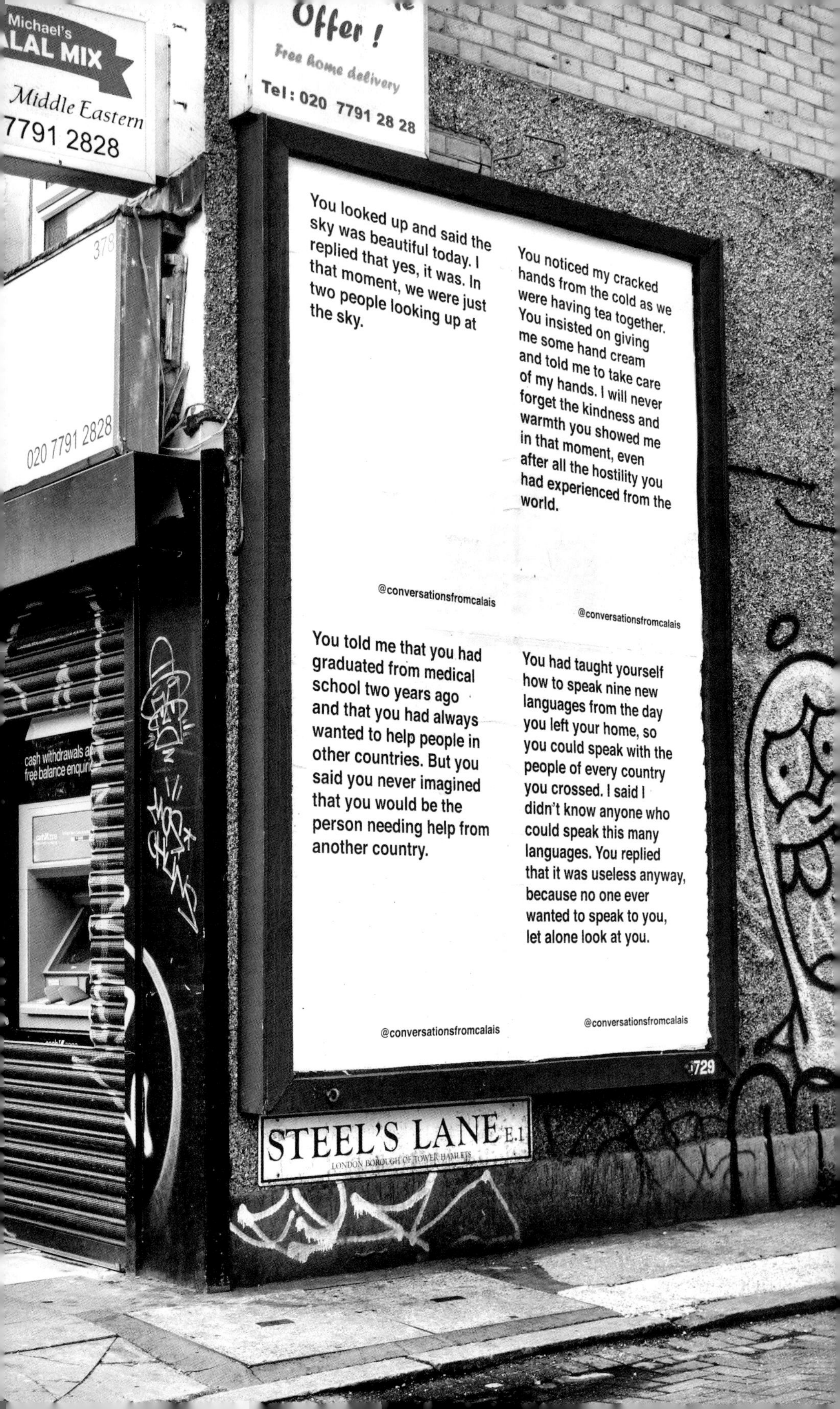
Michael's
ALAL MIX
Middle Eastern
7791 2828
Offer !
Free home delivery
Tel: 020 7791 28 28
020 7791 2828
You looked up and said the sky was beautiful today. I replied that yes, it was. In that moment, we were just two people looking up at the sky.
@conversationsfromcalais
You noticed my cracked hands from the cold as we were having tea together. You insisted on giving me some hand cream and told me to take care of my hands. I will never forget the kindness and warmth you showed me in that moment, even after all the hostility you had experienced from the world.
@conversationsfromcalais
You told me that you had graduated from medical school two years ago and that you had always wanted to help people in other countries. But you said you never imagined that you would be the person needing help from another country.
@conversationsfromcalais
You had taught yourself how to speak nine new languages from the day you left your home, so you could speak with the people of every country you crossed. I said I didn't know anyone who could speak this many languages. You replied that it was useless anyway, because no one ever wanted to speak to you, let alone look at you.
@conversationsfromcalais
STEEL'S LANE E.1
LONDON BOROUGH OF TOWER HAMLETS

ESSAY BY

NISH KUMAR

COMEDIAN & TELEVISION PRESENTER

You noticed my cracked hands from the cold as we were having tea together. You insisted on giving me some hand cream and told me to take care of my hands. I will never forget the kindness and warmth you showed me in that moment, even after all the hostility you had experienced from the world.

@conversationsfromcalais

LESSONS IN KINDNESS

We will all have our personal learnings, but what of the more general societal lessons?

We spent two years locked in our houses to avoid the poisonous air caused by someone getting frisky with a bat. I know, that isn't what happened, but the reality is far too complicated. And it is not the worst misinformation about the pandemic a comedian has delivered – at least I'm not suggesting it can be cured by taking a horse dewormer or contacting an exorcist.

So, if we are done with this particular period of history, then only one question remains: what did you learn?

Personally, I learned two key lessons:

1. A comedian is not a "key worker". Granted, I probably should have already known this. Society is perfectly capable of functioning without comedians. No one in human history will ever utter the words: "Is anyone in here a comedian? It's an emergency."
2. I am capable of making a curry that is not a total insult to my Indian ancestry. Robbed of my usual options of restaurants and takeaways, I pivoted into something I had read about called "cooking". It was pretty good.

We will all have our personal learnings, but what of the more general societal lessons? Here are a few things I think we all learned:

1. When refugees are at a distance, it's easy to be compassionate. Just as it was when we saw the pandemic unfolding in China.
2. The state can transform people's lives far more effectively than rich people. Governments around the world stepped in and paid their citizens' wages. Meanwhile, the richest men on the planet continued to contrive ways to avoid paying their fair share of tax and then got into a contest to try and blast off into space. They may as well have dropped their pants and got out a ruler. Frankly, that would have been more dignified and less environmentally damaging.

Anyone's circumstances can change suddenly and uncontrollably.

3. Anyone's circumstances can change suddenly and uncontrollably. So, perhaps, in future, if you see someone living on the street, or desperate people seeking refuge in a different country, instead of assuming they are only there as a result of poor decision making, consider that things may have happened that were out of their control. For years, we were told that people on unemployment benefits were simply lazy. Then, suddenly, the entire country was unable to work and needed assistance. Things can happen; lives can change in an instant. Start from that assumption when you interact with the world.

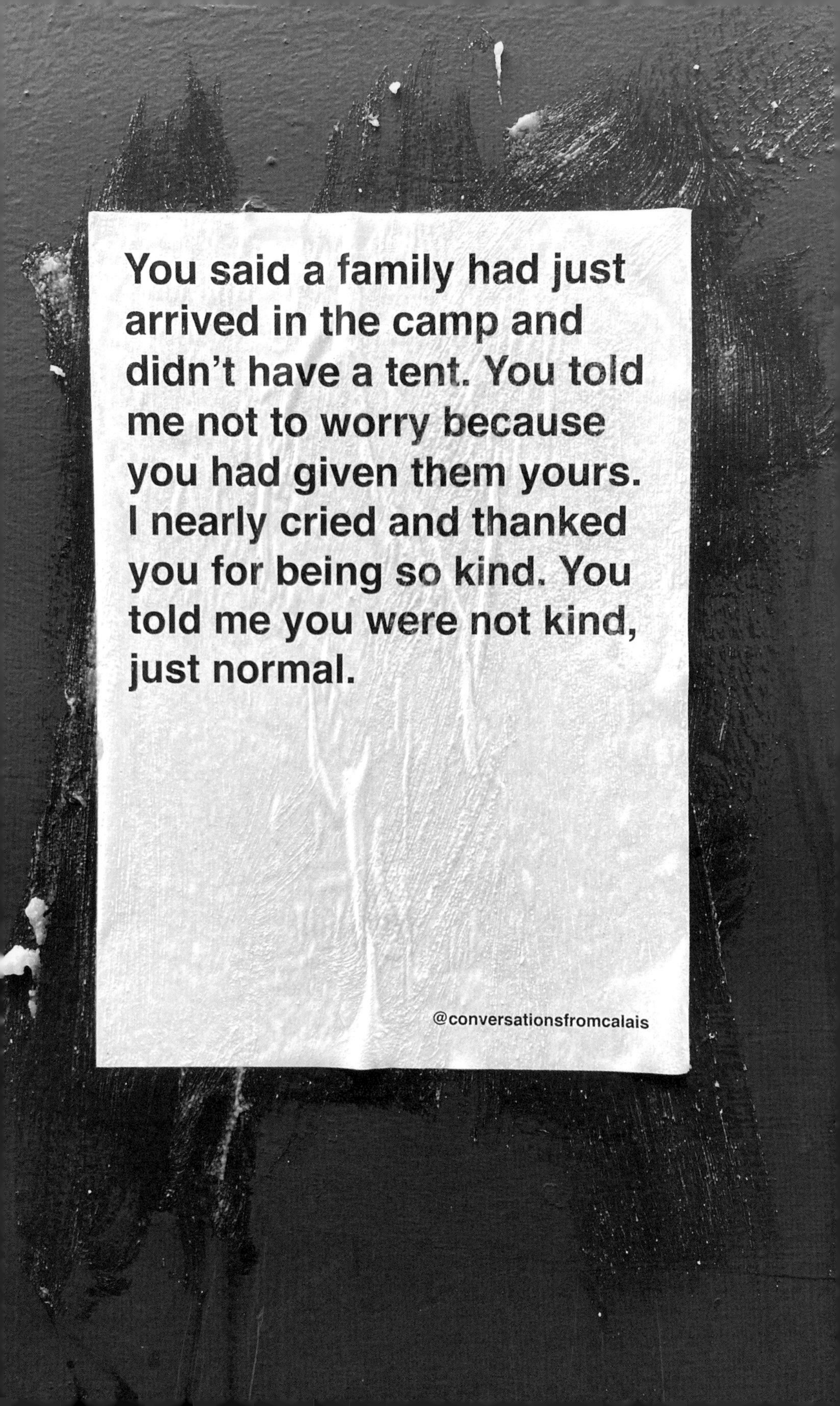

You said a family had just arrived in the camp and didn't have a tent. You told me not to worry because you had given them yours. I nearly cried and thanked you for being so kind. You told me you were not kind, just normal.

@conversationsfromcalais

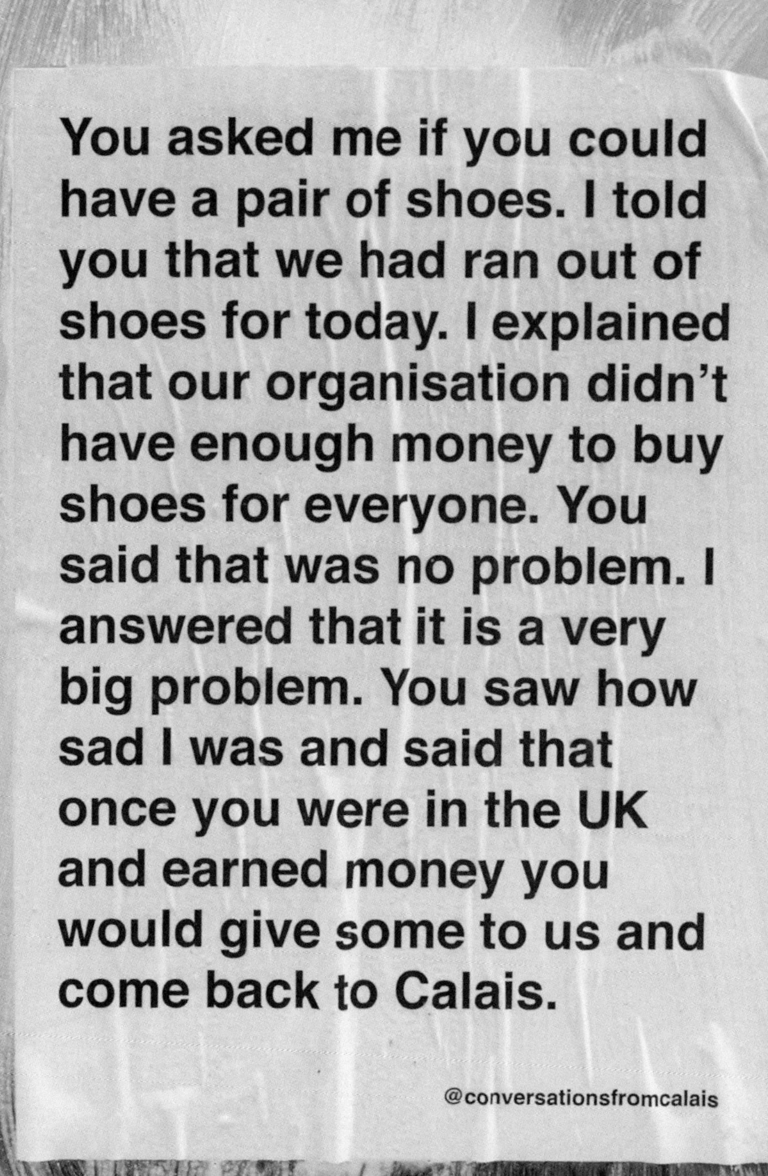
You asked me if you could have a pair of shoes. I told you that we had ran out of shoes for today. I explained that our organisation didn't have enough money to buy shoes for everyone. You said that was no problem. I answered that it is a very big problem. You saw how sad I was and said that once you were in the UK and earned money you would give some to us and come back to Calais.
@conversationsfromcalais

4. Kindness and connection are the only things that matter. During the pandemic, we saw unbelievable acts of kindness. Charity workers staffed food banks. Doctors and nurses went into war zones and, in some cases, gave their lives to protect us. People sought connection by setting up Zoom groups and then, when it was legal, sat across from each other in parks. At points in the depths of winter, everyone pretended it wasn't freezing and their beers hadn't turned into boozy ice lollies.

Kindness and connection are the only things that matter.

As we move forward, we must take the lessons we've learned to heart. To not do that, would be as pointless and as self-sabotaging as one of those rich man space penises.

NISH KUMAR considers himself a mild-mannered British Asian man who does comedy. He is a British stand-up comedian, actor and television presenter. He is best known for performing and presenting topical comedy series such as *Newsjack* and *The Mash Report*, and was nominated for the Foster's Edinburgh Comedy Award in both 2015 and 2016.

nishkumar.co.uk
@mrnishkumar

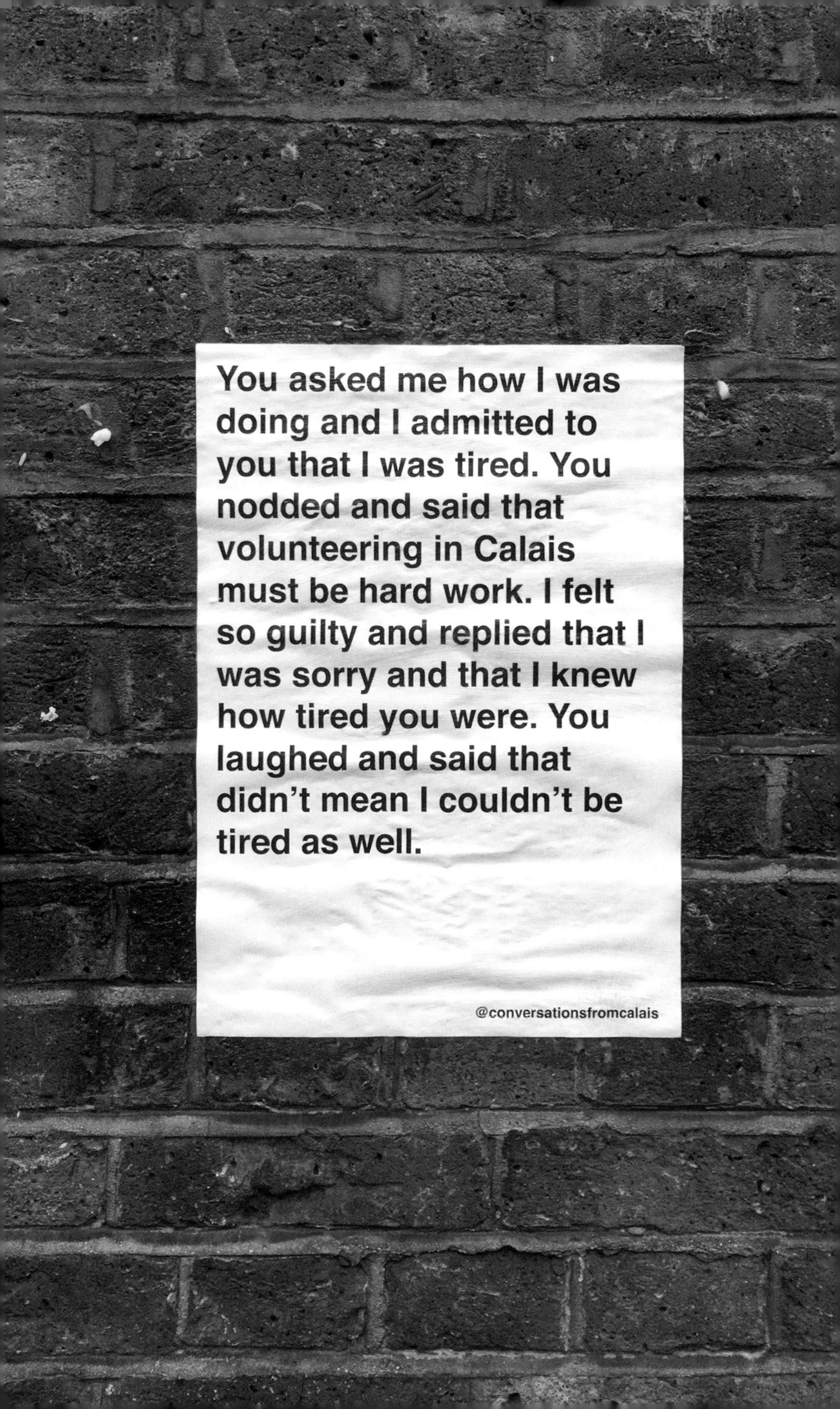
You asked me how I was doing and I admitted to you that I was tired. You nodded and said that volunteering in Calais must be hard work. I felt so guilty and replied that I was sorry and that I knew how tired you were. You laughed and said that didn't mean I couldn't be tired as well.
@conversationsfromcalais

"It's hard to find the right words to talk about Calais. Oftentimes it felt dark and desperate for both volunteers and the people we supported. But what was remarkable were the times when collective humanity shone a light so bright you couldn't help but feel the glow."

SOPHIE, Volunteer

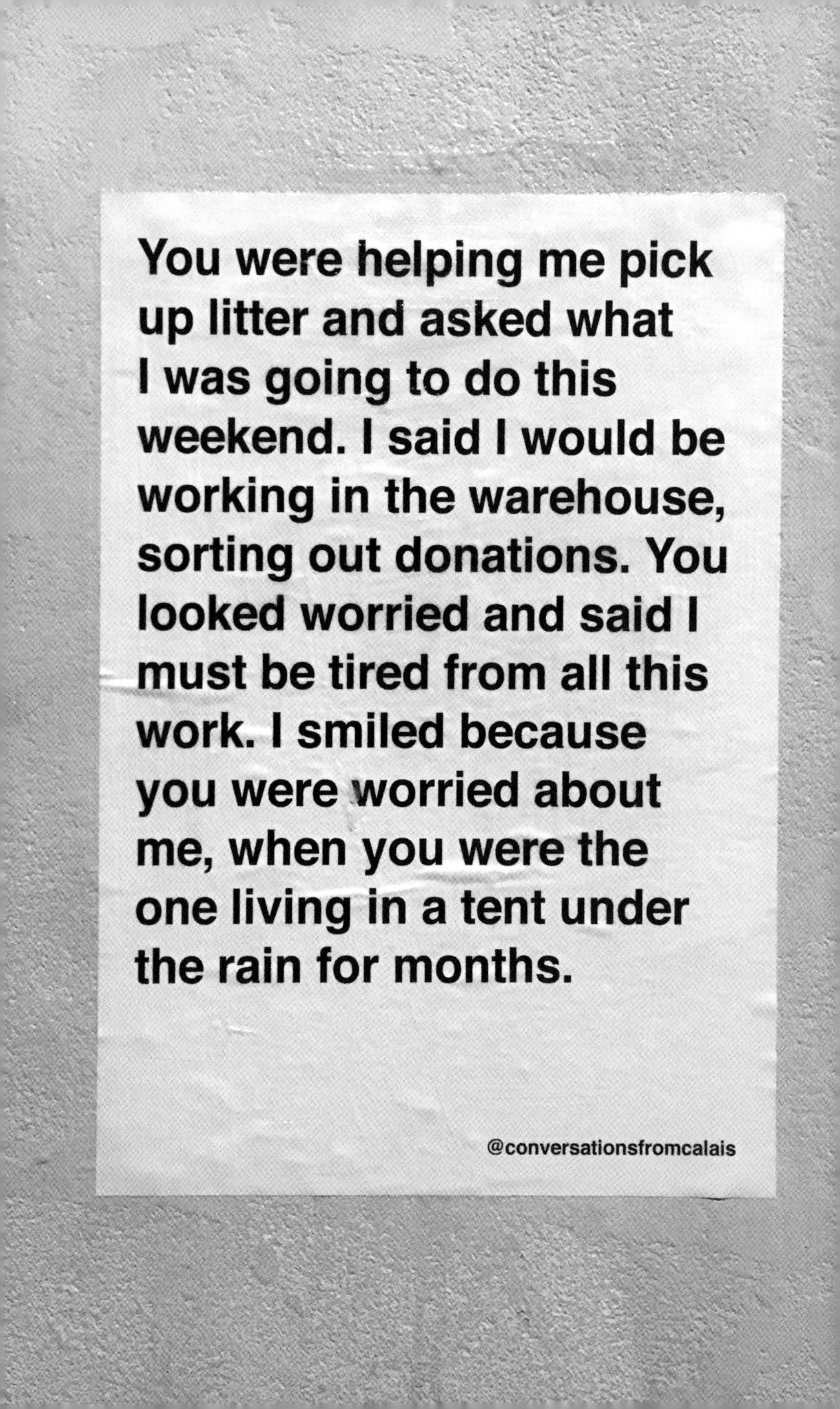

You were helping me pick up litter and asked what I was going to do this weekend. I said I would be working in the warehouse, sorting out donations. You looked worried and said I must be tired from all this work. I smiled because you were worried about me, when you were the one living in a tent under the rain for months.

@conversationsfromcalais

You asked me if I could give my passport to your friend, to get into the UK. I responded that I couldn’t do that, that your friend didn’t look like me at all. Suddenly, we were laughing, comparing our faces. You translated the joke to your friends, who loved it. You said it felt so good to laugh. You said laughing made living in these places bearable.

@conversationsfromcalais

You were eating dinner and I asked you if you liked the food I had made. You answered that it wasn’t great and that yesterday was better. I said I had cooked the food yesterday as well. You said it must have not been that great yesterday either then. We laughed together.

@conversationsfromcalais

"Showcases what the world so desperately needs more of right now: heart, hope and humanity."

EMMA GANNON, Author & podcaster

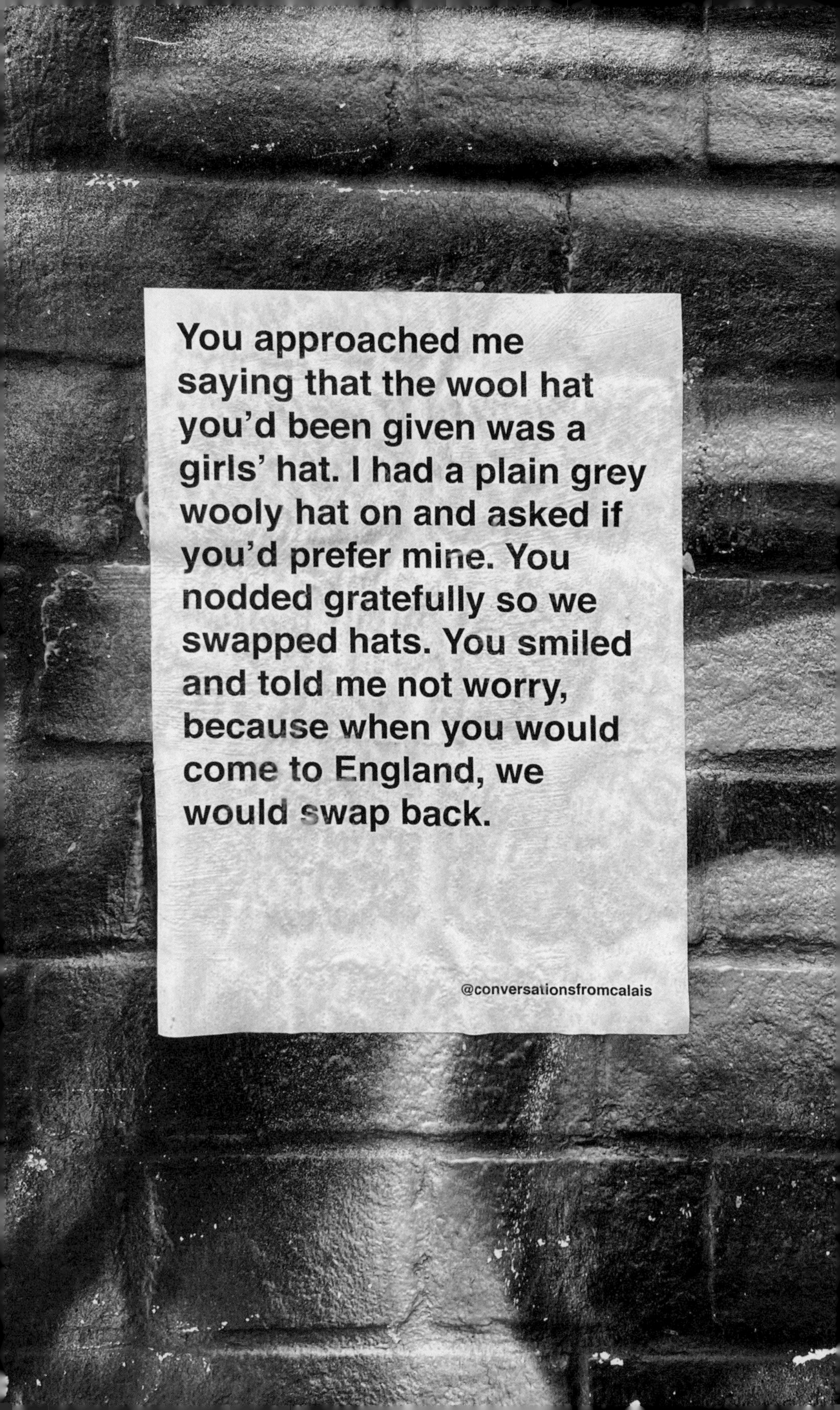

You approached me saying that the wool hat you'd been given was a girls' hat. I had a plain grey wooly hat on and asked if you'd prefer mine. You nodded gratefully so we swapped hats. You smiled and told me not worry, because when you would come to England, we would swap back.

@conversationsfromcalais

You were one of the oldest men in the Sudanese camp. You would always make a fire and serve tea for everyone. You always invited me to have tea with you and we would never drink it unless you were sitting with all of us.

@conversationsfromcalais

You
that when
crossin
he desert your
friend
in your
arms
you
his
So
and

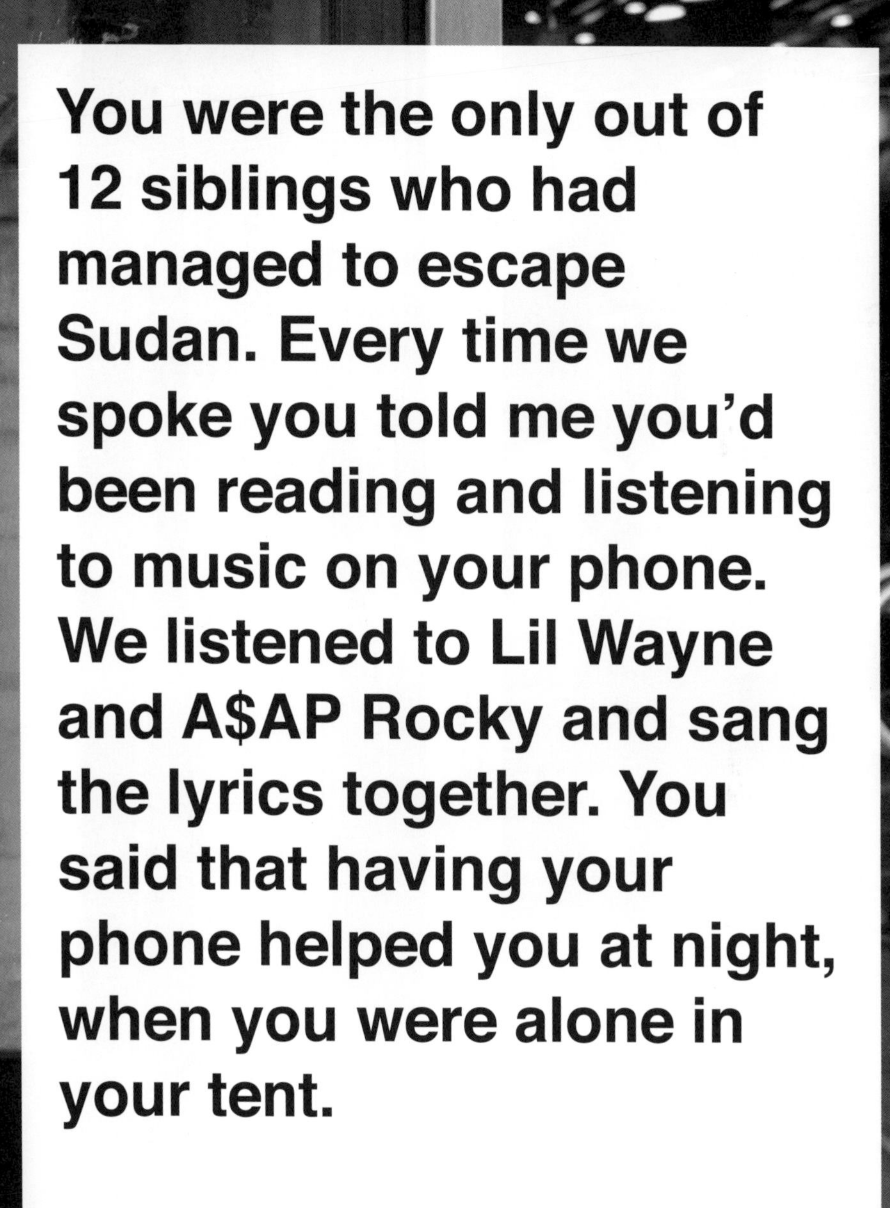
CAMBER
You were the only out of 12 siblings who had managed to escape Sudan. Every time we spoke you told me you'd been reading and listening to music on your phone. We listened to Lil Wayne and A$AP Rocky and sang the lyrics together. You said that having your phone helped you at night, when you were alone in your tent.
@conversationsfromcalais

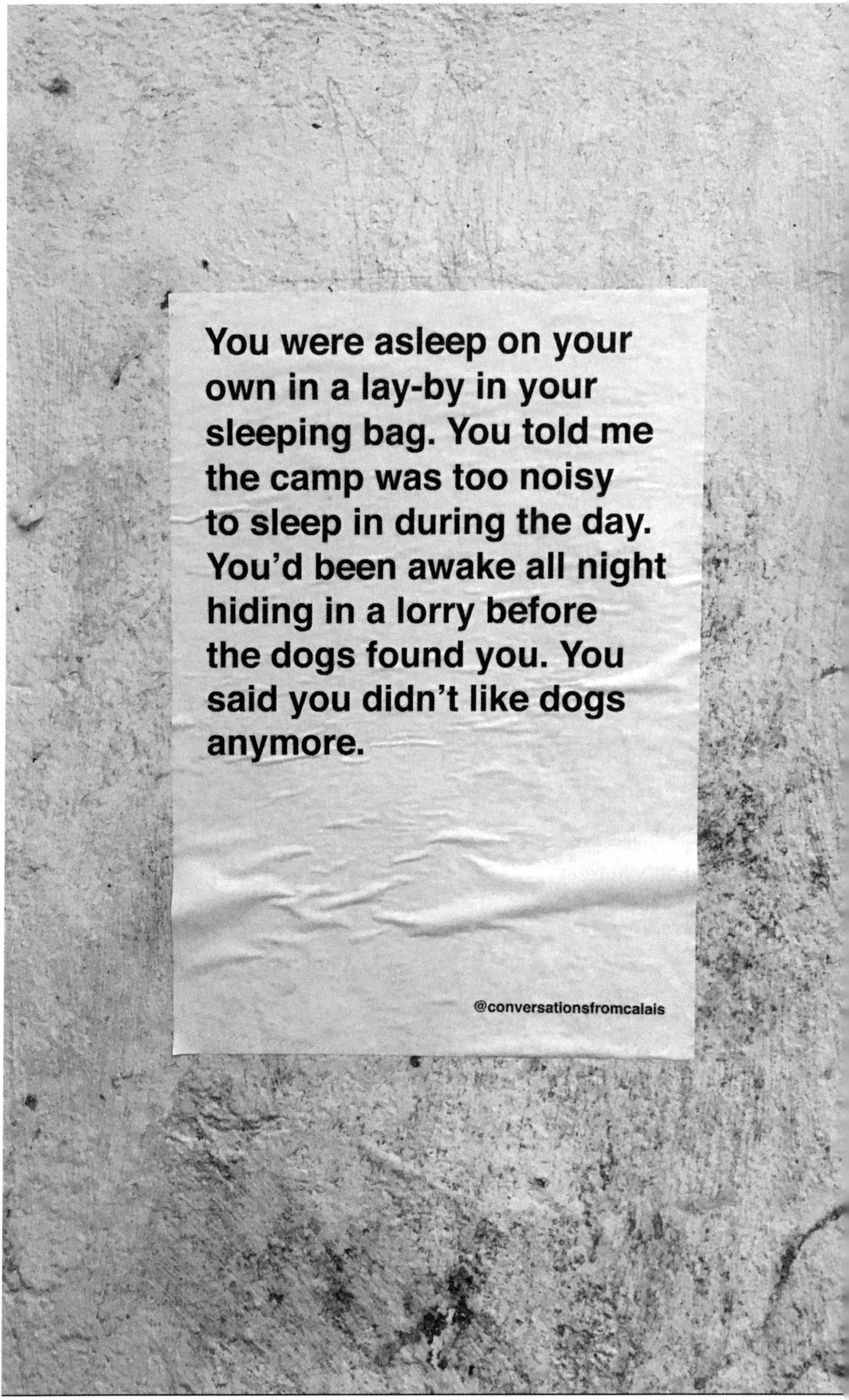

You were asleep on your own in a lay-by in your sleeping bag. You told me the camp was too noisy to sleep in during the day. You'd been awake all night hiding in a lorry before the dogs found you. You said you didn't like dogs anymore.

@conversationsfromcalais

04

FOOD & SHELTER

T/AS
AKDENIZ BAKERY
The Royal Bakery
RTHDAY & WEDDING CAKE ORDERS TAKEN
The Royal Bakery
ANDWICHES & BAGELS
02079234838
You wanted to play football so we walked to the grass and made two teams. As always your team won. I said it was unfair because you were too good at running away with the ball. You said it was unfair because I could run away anywhere in the world a[...] no one would stop me.
You told me you were an Olympian who had been to Rio in 2016, but now you were here and you felt suffocated because you couldn't follow your passion. You said you wanted to coach children and couldn't wait to get your papers.
@conversationsfromcalais
No dogs
7071

ESSAY BY

JOUDIE KALLA

CHEF, AUTHOR & ACTIVIST

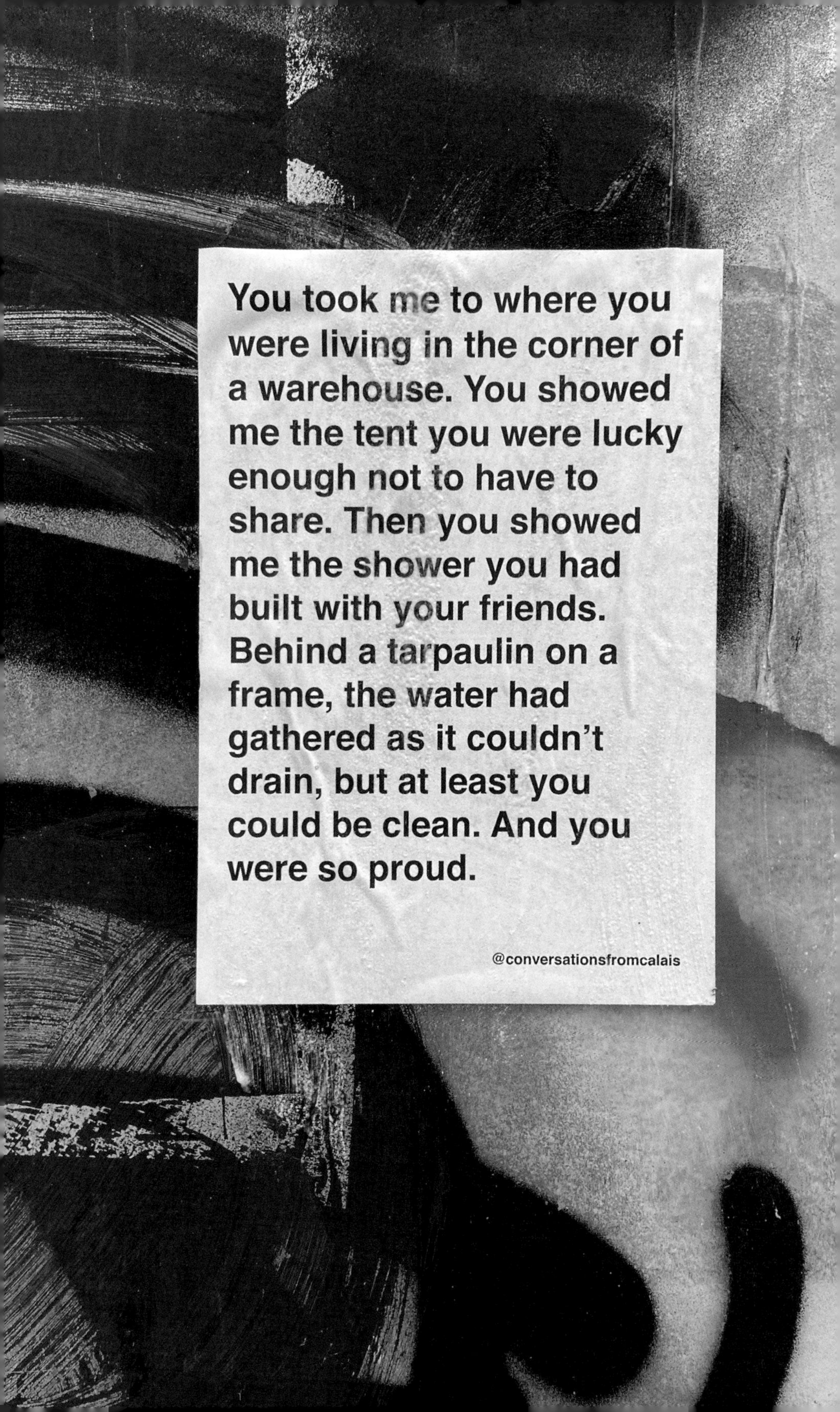
You took me to where you were living in the corner of a warehouse. You showed me the tent you were lucky enough not to have to share. Then you showed me the shower you had built with your friends. Behind a tarpaulin on a frame, the water had gathered as it couldn’t drain, but at least you could be clean. And you were so proud.
@conversationsfromcalais

I AM FROM THERE, I AM FROM HERE, YET I BELONG NOWHERE

I am the daughter of Palestinian refugees who were made homeless by the creation of the state of Israel in 1948. My family fled for their lives, along with 800,000 others. They were told they would be able to return home after a "while", with the keys to their doors in their hands, yet they remain refugees, still holding those keys, living away from their home and their land.

Separation and distance can be rectified by the act of eating, by closing your eyes and going to that place where you feel safe. Wherever that may be.

Under Israeli law, most Palestinians living in the diaspora (now nearly 10 million) have no right to return to the land they lived in for over 4,000 years. The erasure of a whole people is taking place before our eyes, with the longest military occupation in history that seems to have no end. There will never be a good enough answer to justify what has happened and continues to happen.

Palestine was all we had, and we have had to create shelter and re-imagine our lives again and again for the last 74 years, to relive days gone by, to transport ourselves to a different place. One way we have done this is through food and cooking.

ad caught a big f

e lake in Grande

e. You cooked it

en fire and invite

ogether with your

y, to eat it. I enjoy

hospitality a lot a

had never eaten

delicious fish. Yo

d at me strangely,

ing this was defini

Food is memory, it transports us, evoking all kinds of emotions, from sadness to peace, closeness to joy. Separation and distance can be rectified by the act of eating, by closing your eyes and going to that place where you feel safe. Wherever that may be.

Food was home for my family, and it is intertwined in so many ways to the life they lost forever. What my mother taught me about cooking and our traditions, and what her mother taught her about food, remains with us. Food was my connection to my family, and I think I became a chef to uphold centuries worth of stories that have been passed down. Our recipes and culinary traditions are linked to our geography, to the specific areas they come from and to the people that worked the land. That is why it is vital for the intricacies and details of foods to be recorded correctly. The genocide means they are slowly being washed away, along with our people and our homeland.

Being from a refugee background is my backbone, it keeps me upright. It means knowing the reality of adaptation, loss and the lack of belonging fully somewhere.

Food is ancestral, and traditions don't die easily. I always drink a cup of *molokhia* (jute leaf) when I miss my mum, eat stuffed vine leaves when I think of my sister and make *mussakhan* when I remember my auntie. Food is part of our DNA, linking us to the next generations. Dishes that we have prepared for thousands of years is how we share our life stories: breaking bread with strangers, creating communities that intertwine us together in our new homes, creating a new temporary shelter for us wherever we go.

You were chatting with me as a volunteer was going round offering a piece of her chocolate bar to everyone. As soon as she came up to you, you held out your piece to give it to me. You really wanted to be able to give me something. I lied and said that I’d had my piece earlier and pleaded for you to keep it. I felt humbled by your generosity.

@conversationsfromcalais

Even though we long to go back to where we come from, being from a refugee background is my backbone, it keeps me upright. It means knowing the reality of adaptation, loss and the lack of belonging fully somewhere. My roots were made back home in Palestine and they run deep, like our beautiful olive trees.

I became a chef to uphold centuries worth of stories that have been passed down.

We come from somewhere, and her name is Palestine, and that is important to us in every aspect. We must identify and reclaim where we come from to know where we are going. We are the voices of those who are no longer here, speaking on their behalf, reminding people what has happened to us and what continues to happen to us until today, 74 years later. My family, and my grandmothers in particular, would be so proud of what we are achieving after the great sacrifices they suffered, and for this I am honoured to be a Palestinian. We must stand in our power and keep our resilience if we are ever to go back HOME.

JOUDIE KALLA is an author, chef and activist. Focusing her work on amplifying the Palestinian voice globally through food and history, she has written two bestselling cookbooks, *Palestine on a Plate* and *Baladi – Palestine*, based on Palestinian cuisine, and is also a food consultant. Joudie lives and breathes everything Palestine!

palestineonaplate.com
@palestineonaplate

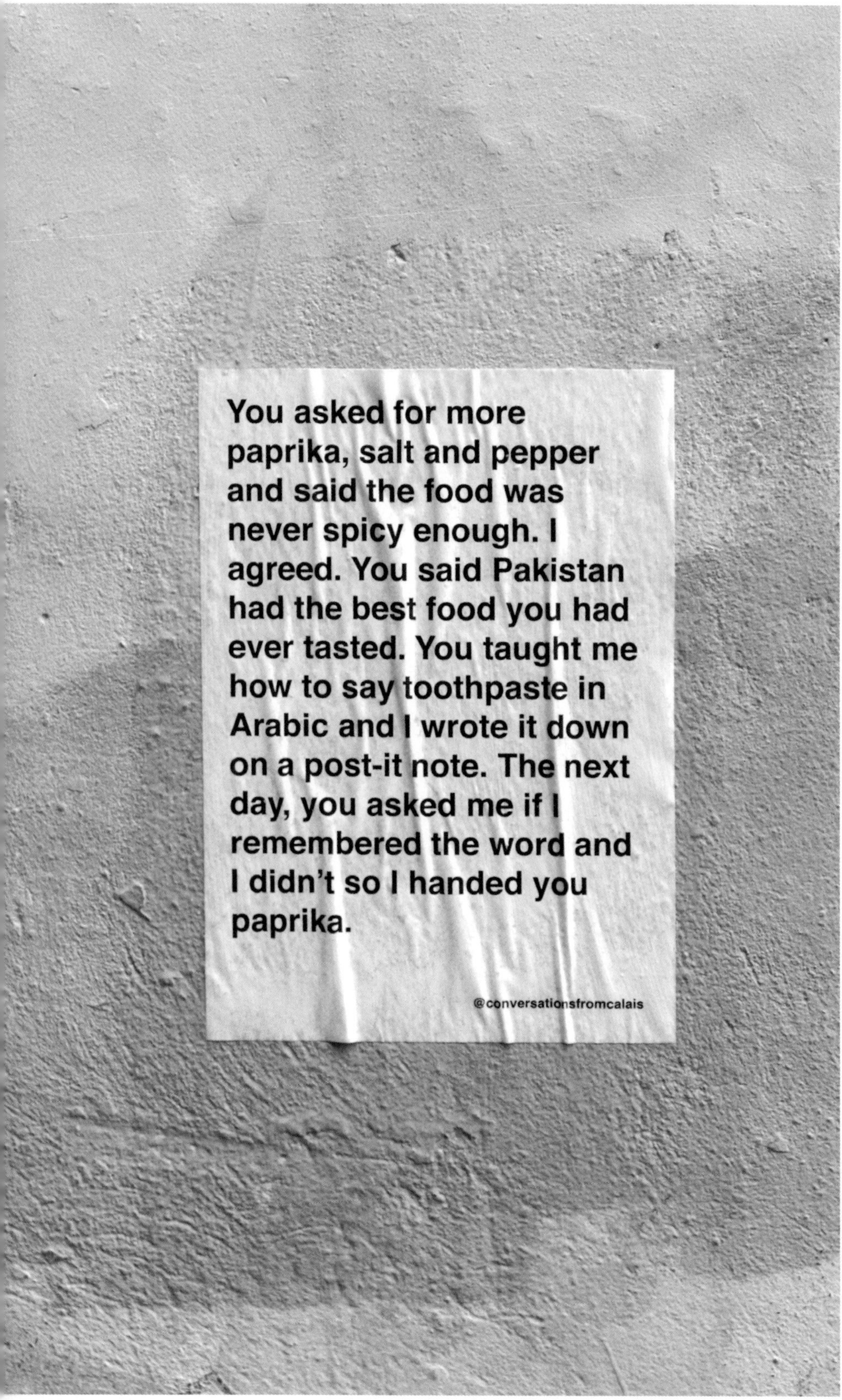

You asked for more paprika, salt and pepper and said the food was never spicy enough. I agreed. You said Pakistan had the best food you had ever tasted. You taught me how to say toothpaste in Arabic and I wrote it down on a post-it note. The next day, you asked me if I remembered the word and I didn't so I handed you paprika.

@conversationsfromcalais

You came up to me and I asked if you could sleep away from the main camp, to avoid the virus. You smiled and said it wasn't possible, after all you were homeless. I felt foolish and powerless. You just shrugged.

@conversationsfromcalais

You talked about your kebab restaurant back home and showed me photos. You were so proud. You flicked through some more, one was just a pile of rubble. You told me this was your shop after a bomb hit it during the war.

@conversationsfromcalais

You were stood in the camp and it was already the third time I had seen you here. You told me you were stuck here. You could not go back and you could not move forward. Once again, I had nothing to offer you but a cup of tea.

@conversationsfromcalais

and pepper
food was
enough. I
said Pakistan
food you had
You t me
bot n
wr wn
ote. next
d r
word and
d you

"Each story I read transports me instantly back to my own days spent in Calais and hits me straight in the heart, in the way that media accounts rarely do. The beautiful thing about these conversations is that you don't have to have personally spent time in Calais to recognise your-selves in them."

RIFAIE TAMMAS, Activist & PhD researcher at the University of Sydney

You asked me why we didn't have any tea or coffee. I said we had to stop serving a lot of things, and change the distribution, because of Corona. You said you had been through so much that Corona could never kill you, and that you would really just like some coffee.

@conversationsfromcalais

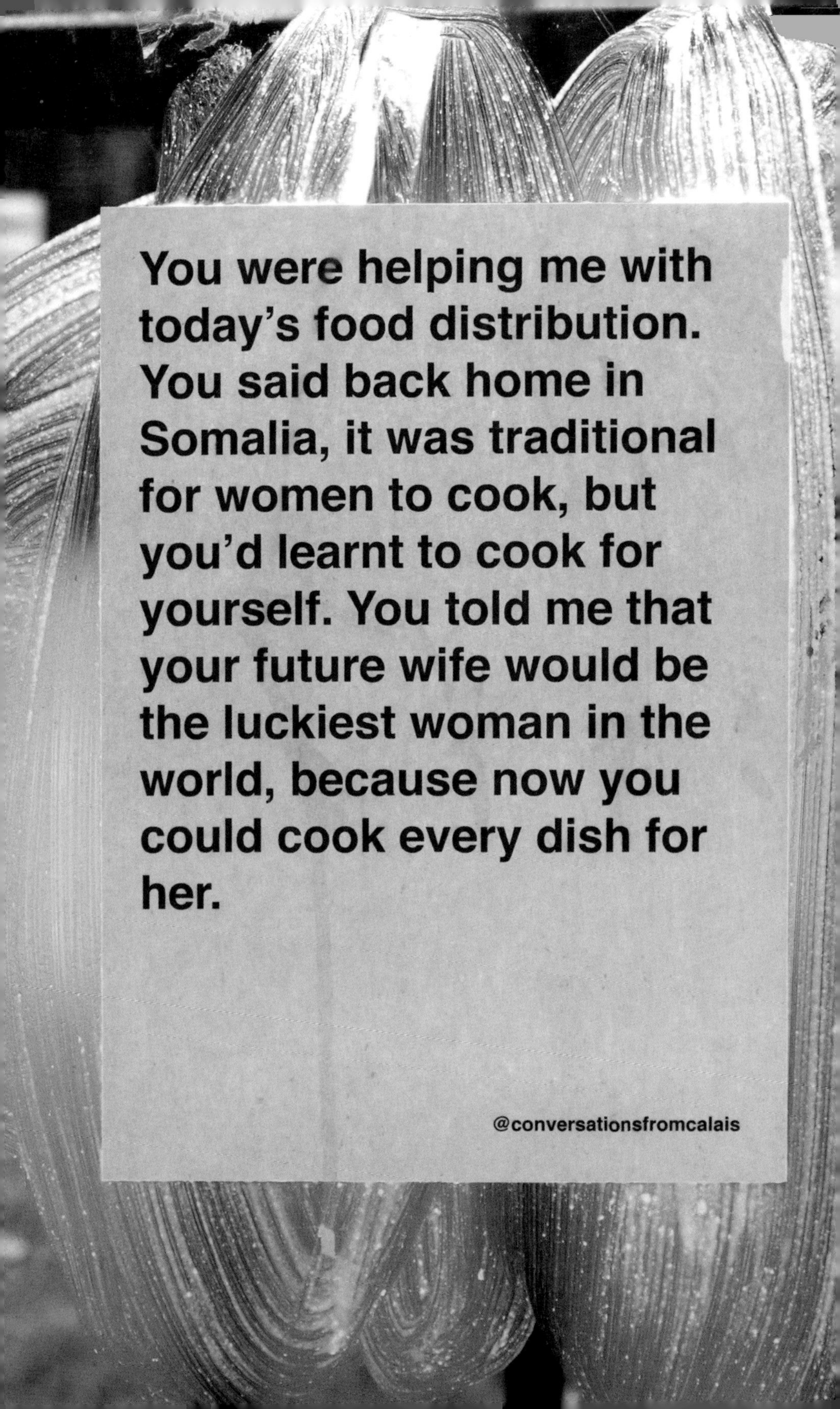

You were helping me with today's food distribution. You said back home in Somalia, it was traditional for women to cook, but you'd learnt to cook for yourself. You told me that your future wife would be the luckiest woman in the world, because now you could cook every dish for her.

@conversationsfromcalais

You saw me as I was picking up rubbish. You said you would help me clean up. I said it was fine, but you answered it upset you that the camp was left so messy because this was your home now. You were responsible for keeping it nice, so you continued to pick up rubbish with me.

@conversationsfromcalais

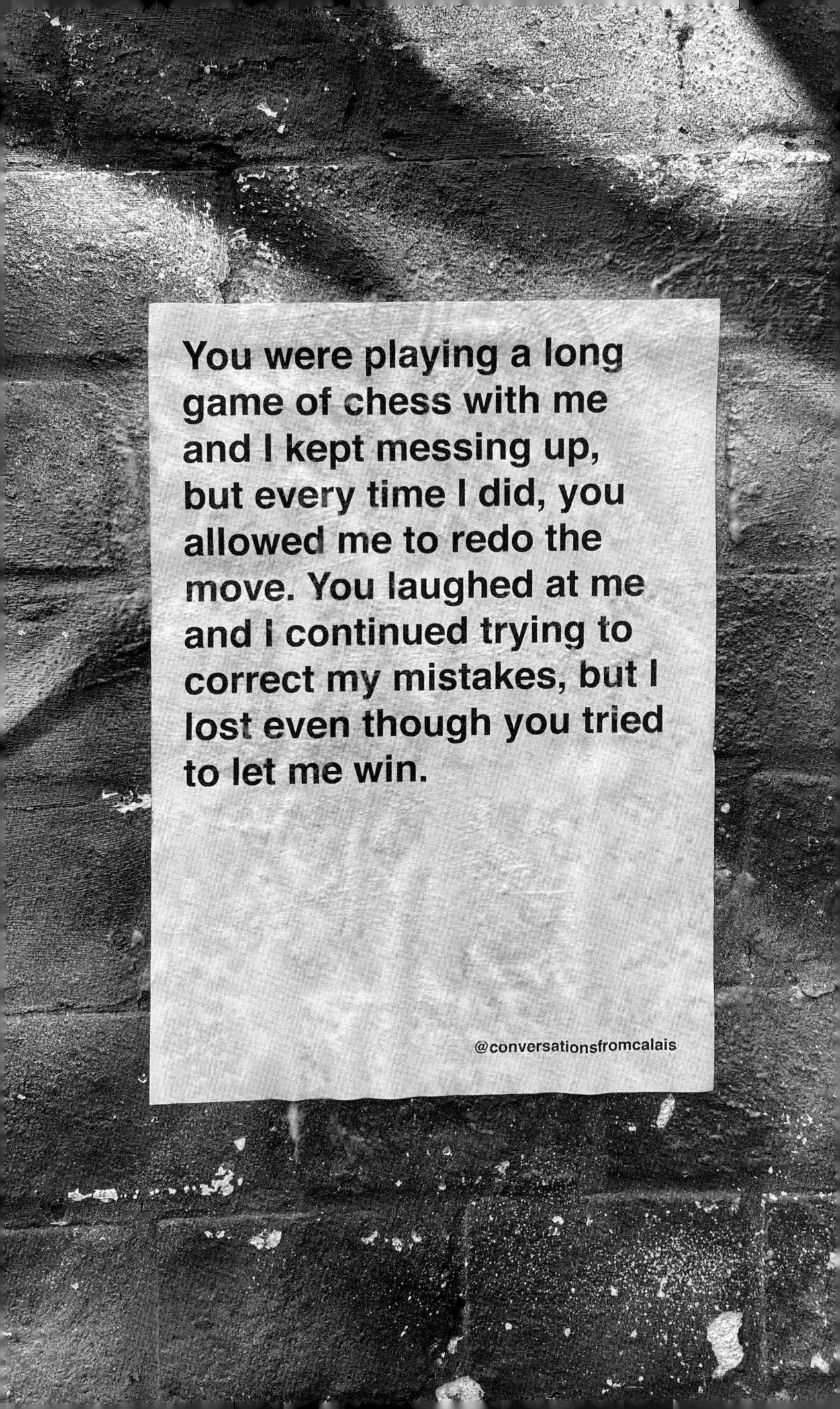

You were playing a long game of chess with me and I kept messing up, but every time I did, you allowed me to redo the move. You laughed at me and I continued trying to correct my mistakes, but I lost even though you tried to let me win.

@conversationsfromcalais

"Broken/ripped donated tents would have their zips fixed and sides sewn up, donated clothing would be mended and patched in an attempt to make them acceptable for another person to wear. Hours of work at sewing machines went into getting zippers back onto tents, all with the aim to of keeping the cold, wind and rain off those sleeping rough outside. I would think of all the time and effort that went into fixing the tents and clothes when I watched the Gendarmerie confiscate those tents and belongings during early morning raids on rough sleeping refugees."

AISLING, Volunteer

You were standing with us as we finished distributing food. We had some bread left, so I asked you if you wanted to take some with you for breakfast the next day. You refused and said you already had some left at your flat. You paused then laughed and said well, at your tent. Though the joke was on you, I couldn't laugh.

@conversationsfromcalais

You had caught a big fish in the lake in Grande Synthe. You cooked it on an open fire and invited me, together with your family, to eat it. I enjoyed your hospitality a lot and said I had never eaten such delicious fish. You all looked at me strangely,

g this was definitely

best fish you had

@conversationsfromcalais

05

LOSS & LONGING

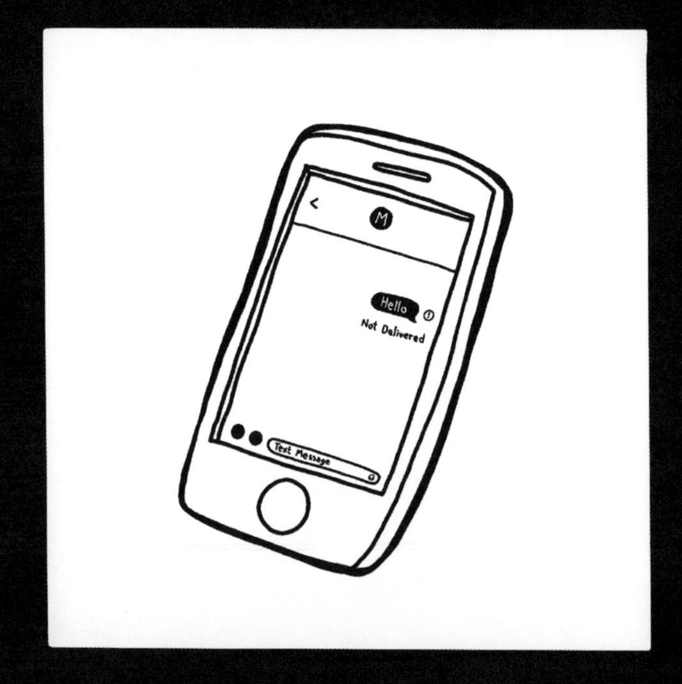

You were sitting on a
bench looking down at
the ground. I sat next to
you and pointed out there
were a lot of ants here.
You laughed and said they
were lucky, because in
Europe animals had better
lives than refugees.
@conversationsfromcalais

ESSAY BY

WAAD AL-KATEAB

FILM-MAKER & ACTIVIST

You told me that you had graduated from medical school two years ago and that you had always wanted to help people in other countries. But you said you never imagined that you would be the person needing help from another country.

@conversationsfromcalais

CHOOSING TO REMEMBER

This terrible situation ended in a scenario we had never considered: forced displacement. It was a shock; there was no time to grieve, nor understand what was happening.

I tried so hard not to think about it. The overwhelming memories I had from Aleppo made every other pain seem unimportant. Stupid even, and silly.

My journey to becoming a refugee didn't happen in a day, or a month, or a single year. Yet, in 2018, I said the words "I want to claim asylum" to the airport authorities; it felt as if I'd left Aleppo just seconds ago. Each word hid the echoes and pictures of what we had been through, and what awaited us was just a blur. Most importantly, a huge part of me was missing: my second daughter Taima, who I had to leave behind …

I had found out in mid-September 2016 that I was pregnant with Taima. It was bad timing, but would there ever have been a good time to conceive in a place where death is a daily reality? East Aleppo had been besieged by Assad forces – Russian and Iranian armies – for 62 days. We had no idea how long it would last, or whether we would survive.

Two months later, this terrible situation ended in a scenario we had never considered: forced displacement. It was a shock; there was no time to grieve, or understand what was happening. There was not even enough time to say goodbye, to anything. To our home, to our loved ones buried there, to the places we loved, to our whole life and memories.

We couldn't even take much with us. But I remember that feeling … how I wished I could take everything. Everything I touched, everything I saw – the trees, the rocks, the smell. Everything.

The road to healing is long and difficult. Forgetting may be one way to get there, but it's not the path I have chosen. I want to remember, and try my best to make up for each minute we were forced to be apart, to live fully with precious moments of love and joy.

In our final few minutes, I went to my house; the first home my husband and I had created together. I cried my eyes out there. I didn't want to leave, but there was no choice. I took some of our plants with me, in the hope that they would grow outside of Aleppo. The thought of saving something from home comforted me while we were waiting to leave, but the plants didn't make it. In the -3-degree temperature they froze and died. Yet I survived, as did my husband Hamza and my daughter Sama. And I felt something immense and precious restored within me while we were exiled in Turkey. Five months later, Taima, my beautiful daughter was born healthy and safe.

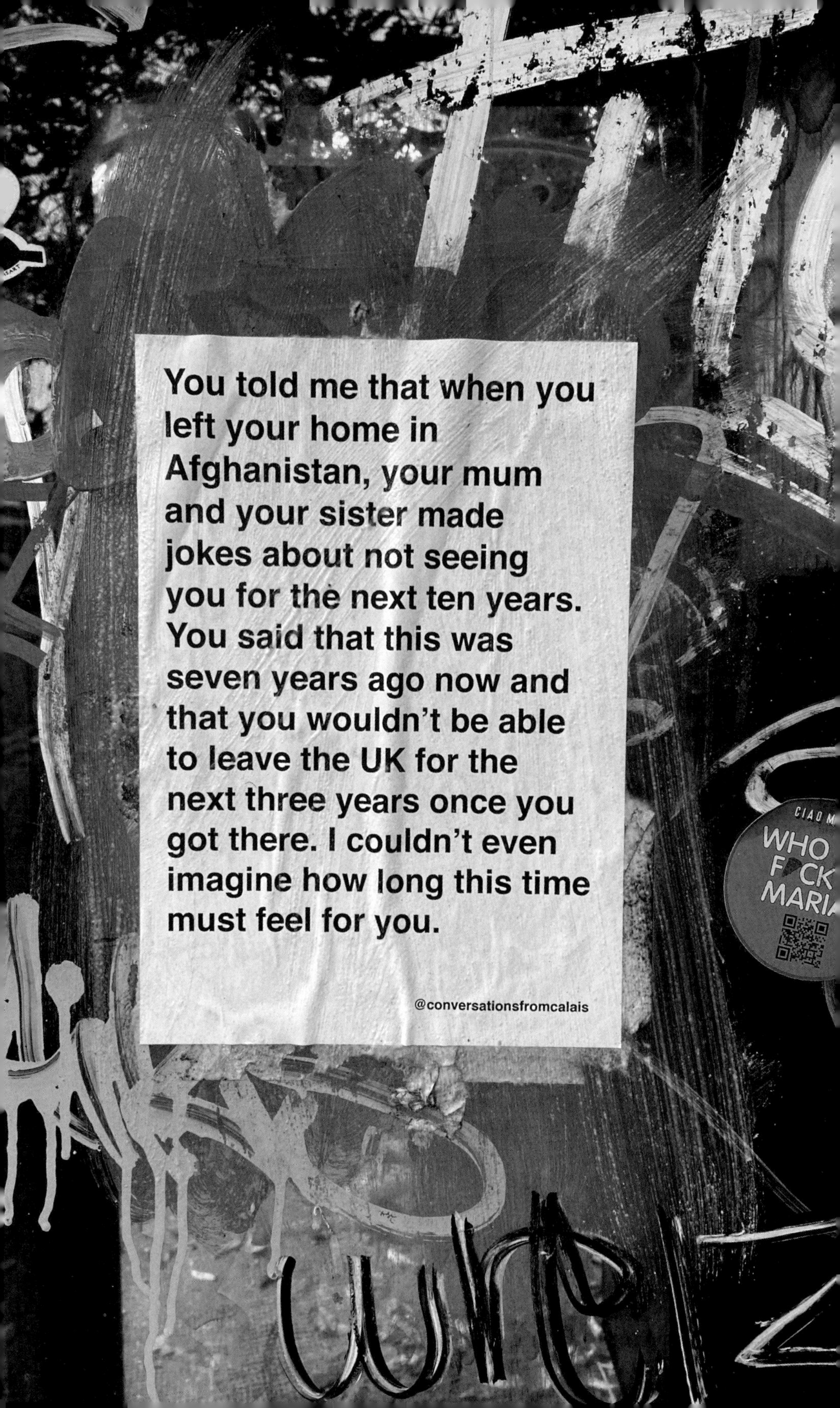
You told me that when you left your home in Afghanistan, your mum and your sister made jokes about not seeing you for the next ten years. You said that this was seven years ago now and that you wouldn't be able to leave the UK for the next three years once you got there. I couldn't even imagine how long this time must feel for you.
@conversationsfromcalais

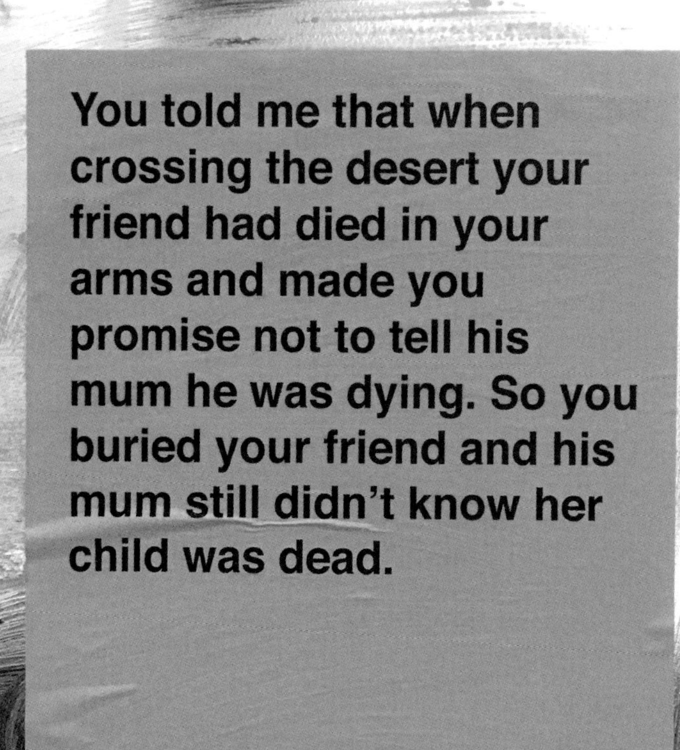
You told me that when crossing the desert your friend had died in your arms and made you promise not to tell his mum he was dying. So you buried your friend and his mum still didn't know her child was dead.
@conversationsfromcalais

As with any Syrian newborn baby, Taima had no formal papers. We tried registering her, but the regime wanted us to go and make the claim personally. It was definitely not an option for us to meet with the regime that was responsible for our displacement. It would have given them the easiest way to arrest us, to kill us directly.

I didn't want to leave, but there was no choice.

Yet, when Taima turned one, because she had no papers I had to make the heartbreaking decision to leave her behind, to seek safety and a better life for her and her sister, for all of us. Every minute of the five months I spent waiting for my papers to be processed – just to be able to go to Turkey and bring her to the UK, to the new home we had created and to be a family again – was a living hell. After the loss of our homeland, to be forced apart from our baby was not a single trauma – it was double, then triple. There are no words that can explain the loss and pain.

The road to healing is long and difficult. Forgetting may be one way to get there, but it's not the path I have chosen. I want to remember, and try my best to make up for each minute we were forced to be apart, to live fully with precious moments of love and joy.

WAAD AL-KATEAB is a Syrian activist and award-winning film-maker. She became a citizen journalist in 2011, after protests broke out across Syria against the Assad regime. Waad's first feature documentary, *For Sama*, documented her life over five years in Aleppo. The film received worldwide critical acclaim, winning numerous awards, including the L'Œil d'or for best documentary at the Cannes Film Festival, Best Documentary at the BAFTAs and a nomination at the 2020 Academy Awards.

actionforsama.com
@actionforsama
@waadalkateab

You asked me why I was here if I had a family, a home and a good life in Ireland. You said I had everything you hoped for and asked why I chose to leave it all behind. You said you knew volunteers weren't bad people but it confused you that we had a life we were leaving behind, when it was the life you wished for everyday.

@conversationsfromcalais

"Each snippet of conversation tells a story of a home lost, a life disrupted, dreams punctured. In direct, often poignant words, the posters bear witness to the diverse experiences of the residents of 'the jungle', and give voice to immigrants and asylum seekers whose stories are so often silenced or unheard."

KHALED HOSSEINI, **International bestselling author of *The Kite Runner***

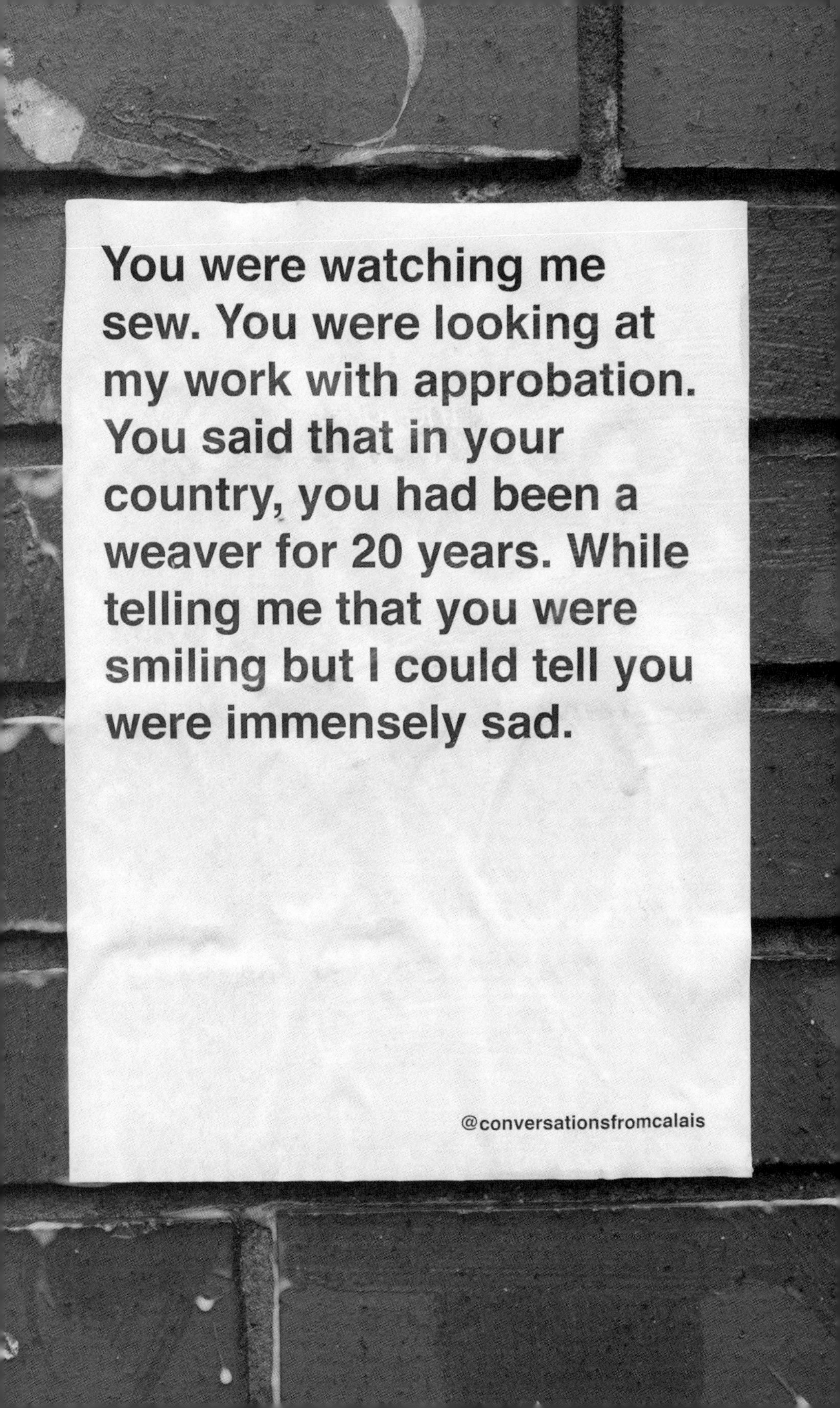

You were watching me sew. You were looking at my work with approbation. You said that in your country, you had been a weaver for 20 years. While telling me that you were smiling but I could tell you were immensely sad.

@conversationsfromcalais

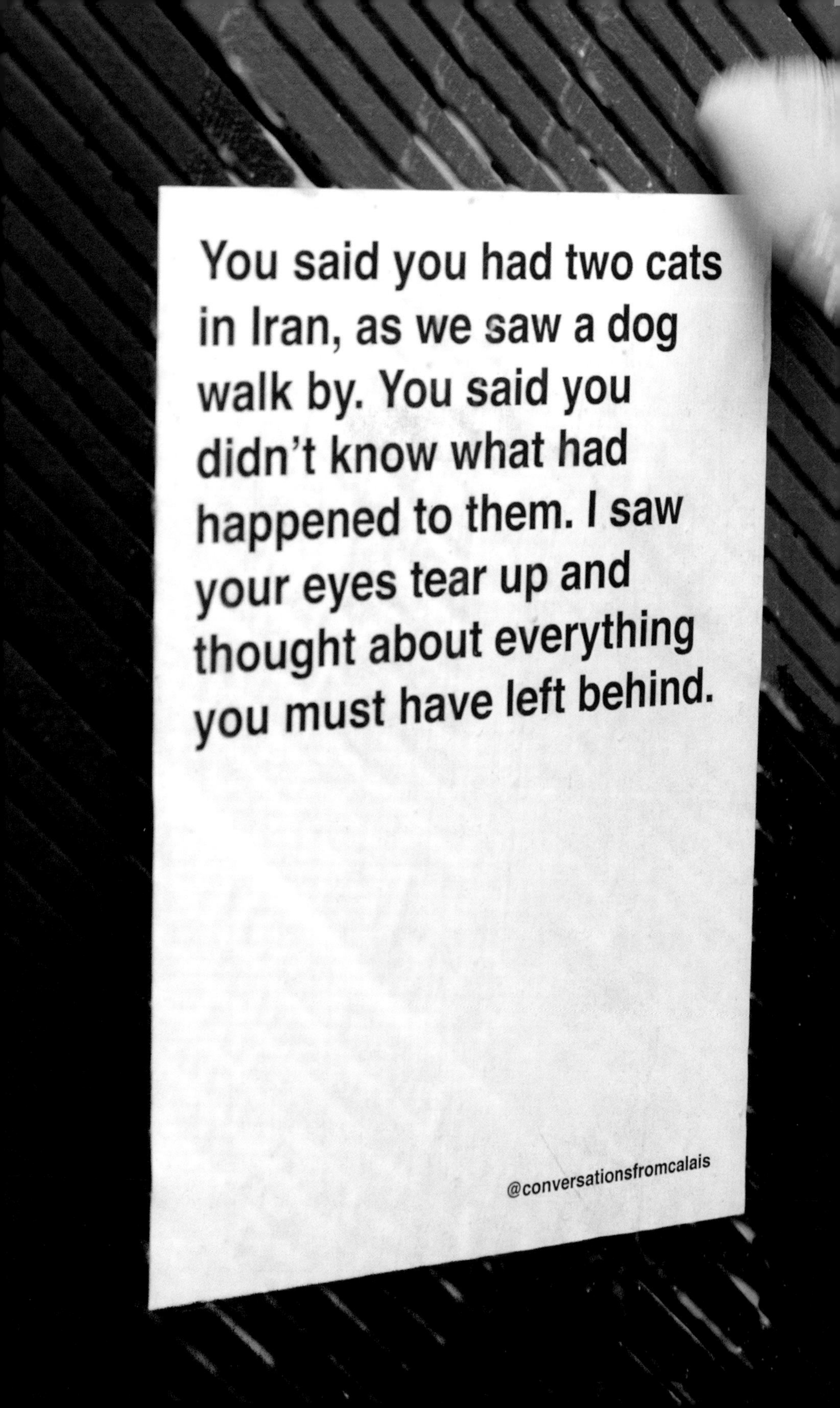

You said you had two cats in Iran, as we saw a dog walk by. You said you didn't know what had happened to them. I saw your eyes tear up and thought about everything you must have left behind.

@conversationsfromcalais

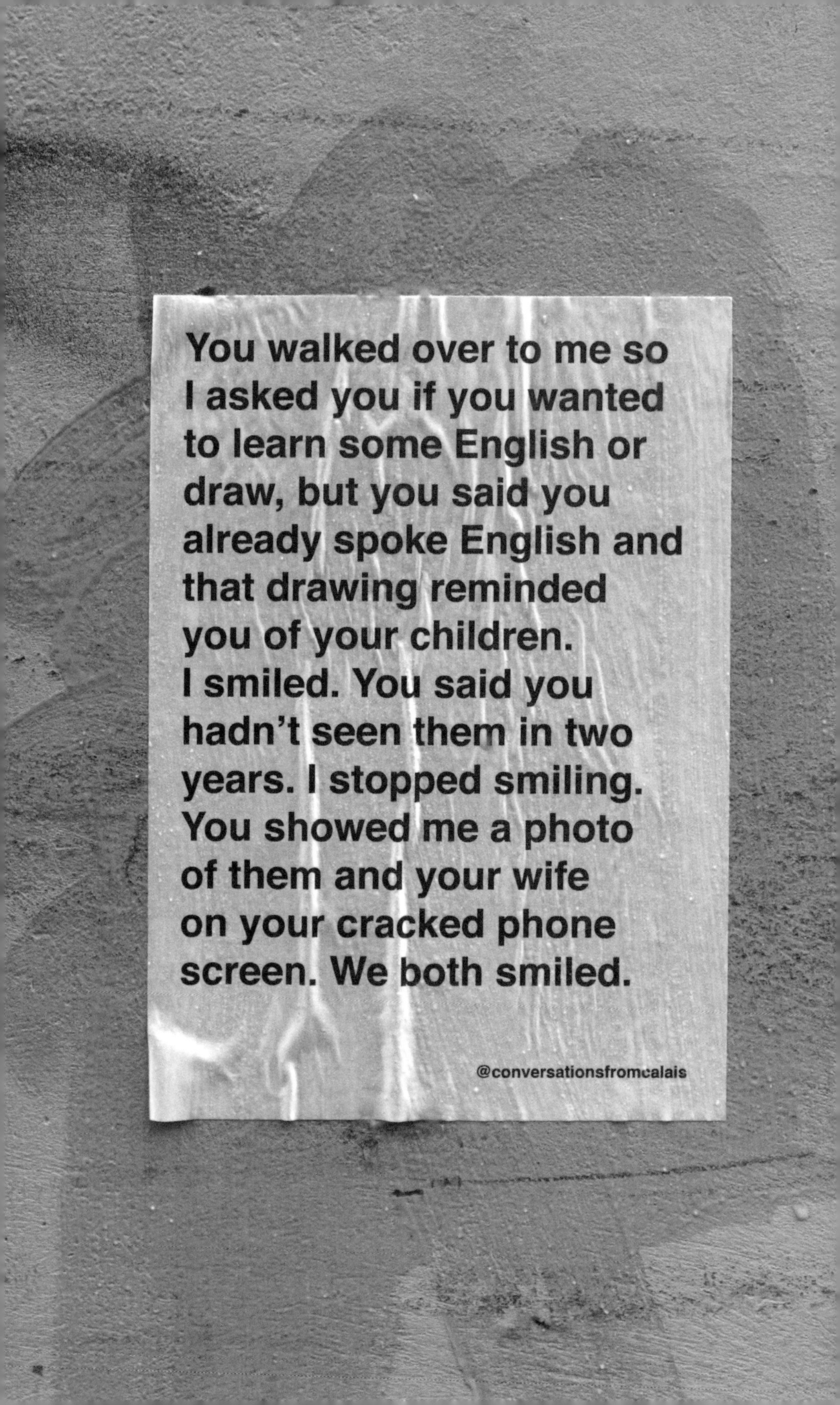

You walked over to me so
I asked you if you wanted
to learn some English or
draw, but you said you
already spoke English and
that drawing reminded
you of your children.
I smiled. You said you
hadn't seen them in two
years. I stopped smiling.
You showed me a photo
of them and your wife
on your cracked phone
screen. We both smiled.

@conversationsfromcalais

"The majority of the people I met in Calais were no different than any other group of people. They loved the sunshine and disliked sleeping out in the rain on cold nights. They took pleasure in plating their foods a certain way and made sure to stop by the spice table in case the food was bland. These were just normal human beings in abnormal conditions. They, in themselves, weren't special or different. They simply found themselves in a situation they no longer wanted to live in. Whether this was due to civil war, poverty or a lack of opportunity, they had a very obvious goal – to find a better life for themselves and their families. And who could fault them for that."

OMAR, Volunteer

You showed me an article
on your phone from a few
months ago about some
refugees found alive in a
refrigerated truck in
Belgium. You told me
brother was one of
said I couldn't
how horrible it
been to be in
You said
worse to
Calais, with no
anywhere.
onto a
was all you hoped
@conversationsfromcalais

You told me you had lost six of your friends in Libya. I told you how deeply sorry I was for your loss. You just smiled at me and said that it was okay, that this was life. I didn't know how to answer.

@conversationsfromcalais

You told me in Iran the pomegranates were sweeter and the flowers brighter. You drew a rose and wrote it in Farsi, so I taught you how to say the colours in French. You said drawing was easier and that it helped you remember. I said it helped me not to forget. You said red was your favourite colour, but that Iran had lost all its colour.

@conversationsfromcalais

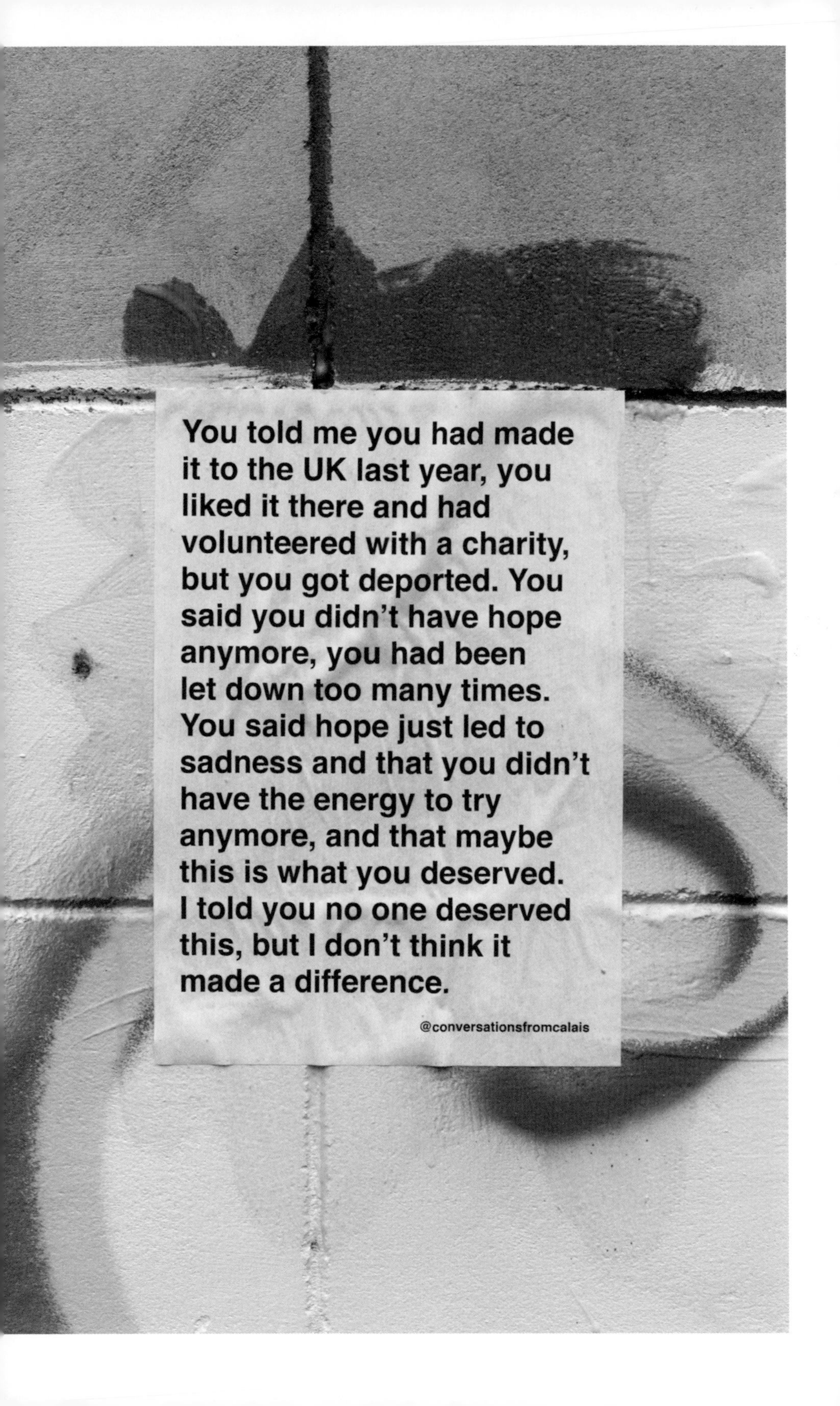
You told me you had made it to the UK last year, you liked it there and had volunteered with a charity, but you got deported. You said you didn't have hope anymore, you had been let down too many times. You said hope just led to sadness and that you didn't have the energy to try anymore, and that maybe this is what you deserved. I told you no one deserved this, but I don't think it made a difference.
@conversationsfromcalais

06

ONFLICT &
SAFETY

You said the government
had stopped bringing
breakfast to the camps
because they were scared
of Corona. You said they
didn't care whether you
died of Corona or hunger,
they just wanted you dead.

ESSAY BY

YASMIN ALIBHAI-BROWN

JOURNALIST & COLUMNIST

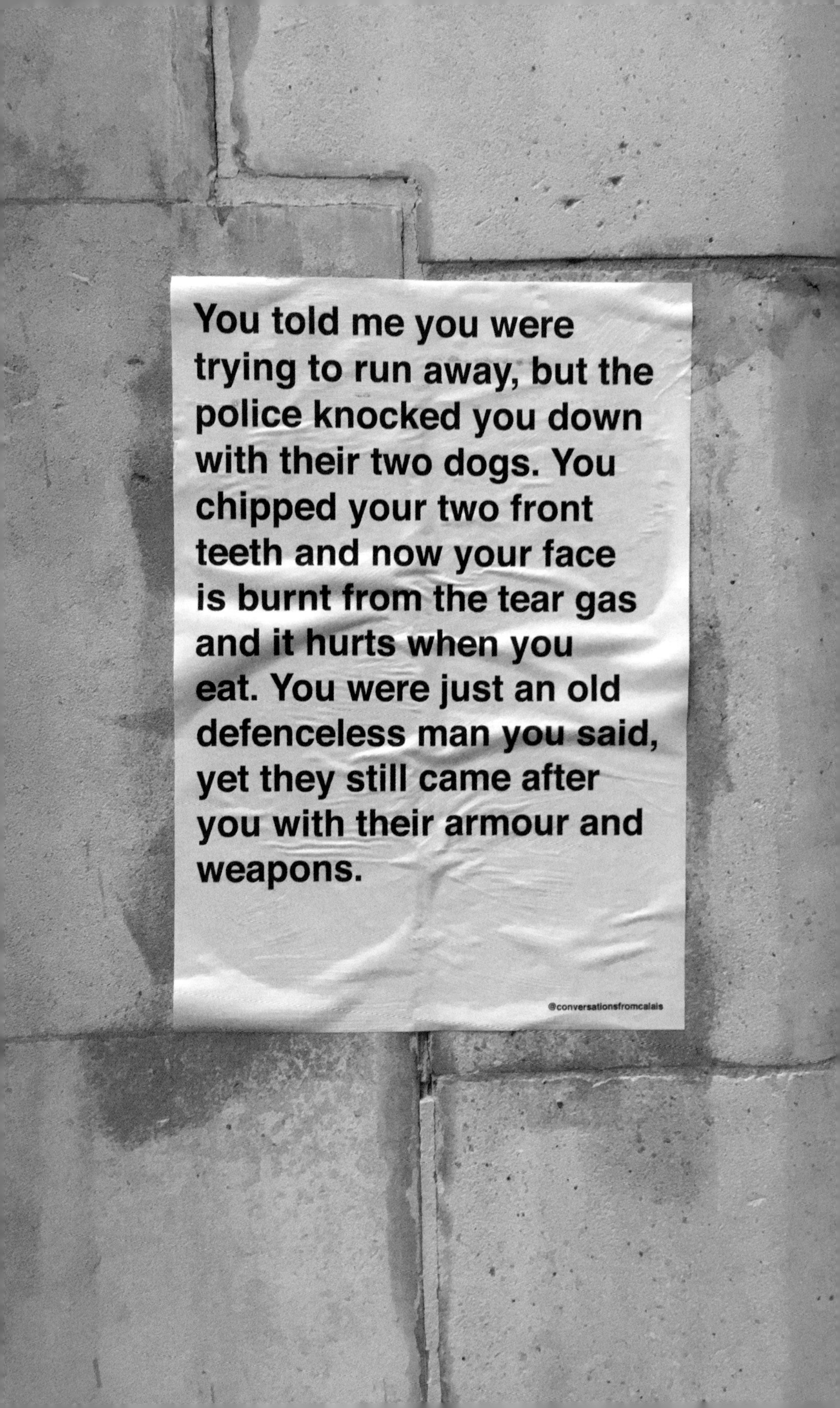

You told me you were trying to run away, but the police knocked you down with their two dogs. You chipped your two front teeth and now your face is burnt from the tear gas and it hurts when you eat. You were just an old defenceless man you said, yet they still came after you with their armour and weapons.

@conversationsfromcalais

UNRESOLVED CONFLICTS & THE UNSETTLED MIGRANT MIND

In May 1972, I landed in Britain, a young woman of 23, my head filled with myths about the "Motherland", her unsurpassed eminence and unrivalled power. Every child raised in the British Empire was thus indoctrinated. It was done so naturally, so smoothly, that few, if any, queried the purveyors, some of whom were black or brown. (Such loyalists still exist. Many have risen high in the Conservative Party in recent years.)

I had a postgraduate scholarship to the University of Oxford. Until we were disabused, we Ugandan Asians believed Britain was the heart of greatness, an orderly genteel haven, the antithesis of African mayhem. It turned out to be anything but genteel and orderly.

Fifty years after resettling here, obnoxious racists still tell me to go back to where I came from, and millions of native Brits remain utterly ignorant about their own history.

Beneath the surface, old conflicts rage on.

British imperialists transported the first Indians to East Africa in the late Victorian age. They were indentured labourers – poorly paid, illiterate workers brought over to build a railway from the coast to the interior. An unknown number died.

The next wave of Indians were small shopkeepers and adventurers seeking to make their fortunes in untapped markets. Colonial administrators soon set up a race- and class-based social structure – whites at the top, browns in the middle, blacks at the bottom. Conflict between peoples of colour was thus institutionalized.

In the 1960s, the decade of African liberation, Asians were offered British citizenship. While some chose to commit to the new nations, the majority rushed to become Her Majesty's subjects, unaware we were volunteering for abysmally low status within a strict caste system. This virtual empire assuaged British national vanity. They lost lands but kept subjects.

Asians had come to believe they were superior to blacks, who now had power in their unforgiving hands. Vengeance and retribution prowled; racist black politicians scapegoated Asians. Tensions between brown and black in East Africa continue to this day.

This was the Cold War era. Marxist socialism was gaining influence across East Africa. Asians, natural born capitalists, propped up the economy. Those who could, began to emigrate to Britain. They included the parents of Priti Patel, Rishi Sunak and Suella Braverman. As numbers grew, Enoch Powell condemned the influx. His popularity soared.

In 1968, the Labour government hastily passed a new immigration law strictly limiting the entry into the UK of East African British Asians. *The Times* condemned the Act: "[The Labour Party] does not … believe in the equality of British citizens. It believes in the equality of white citizens."

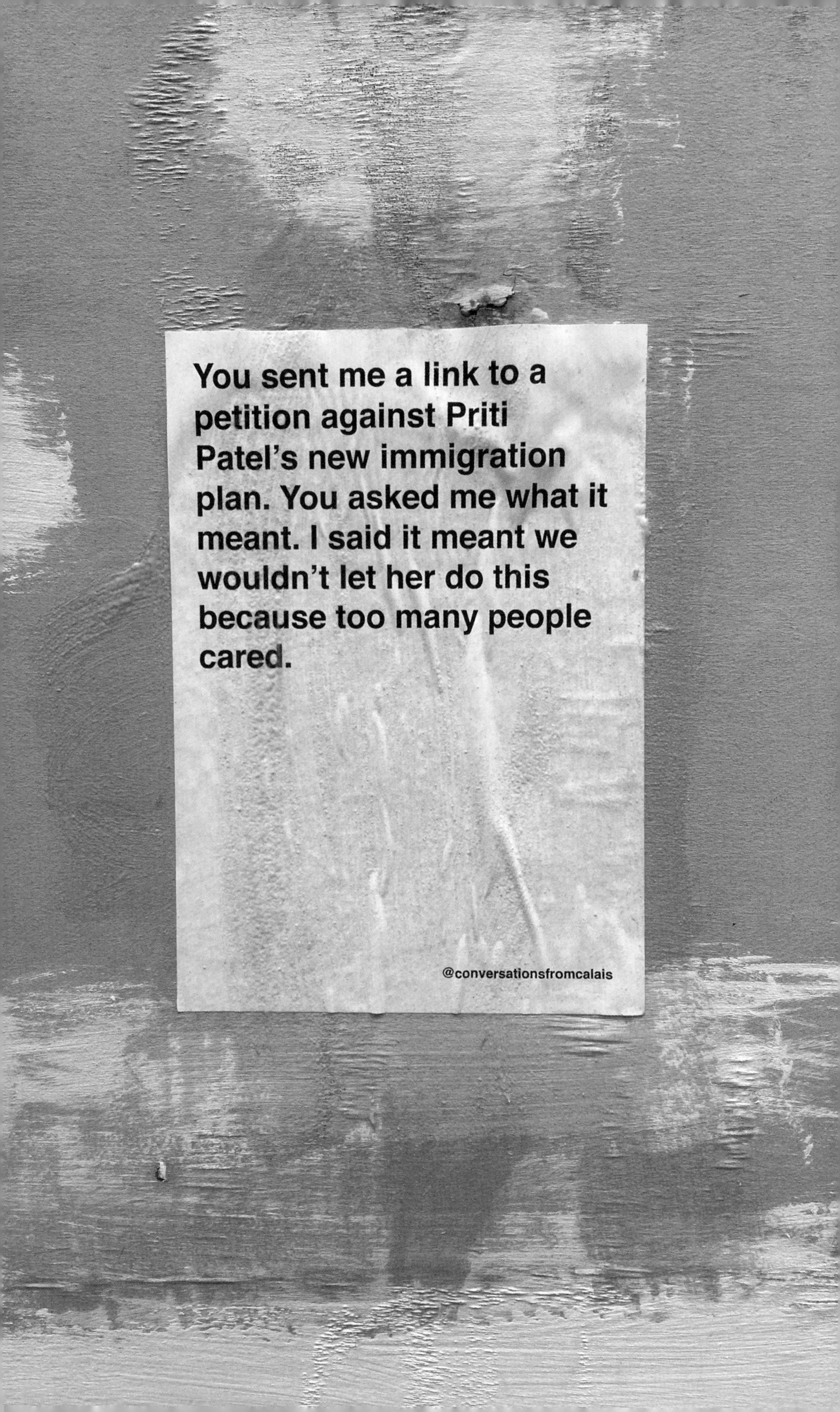

You sent me a link to a petition against Priti Patel's new immigration plan. You asked me what it meant. I said it meant we wouldn't let her do this because too many people cared.

@conversationsfromcalais

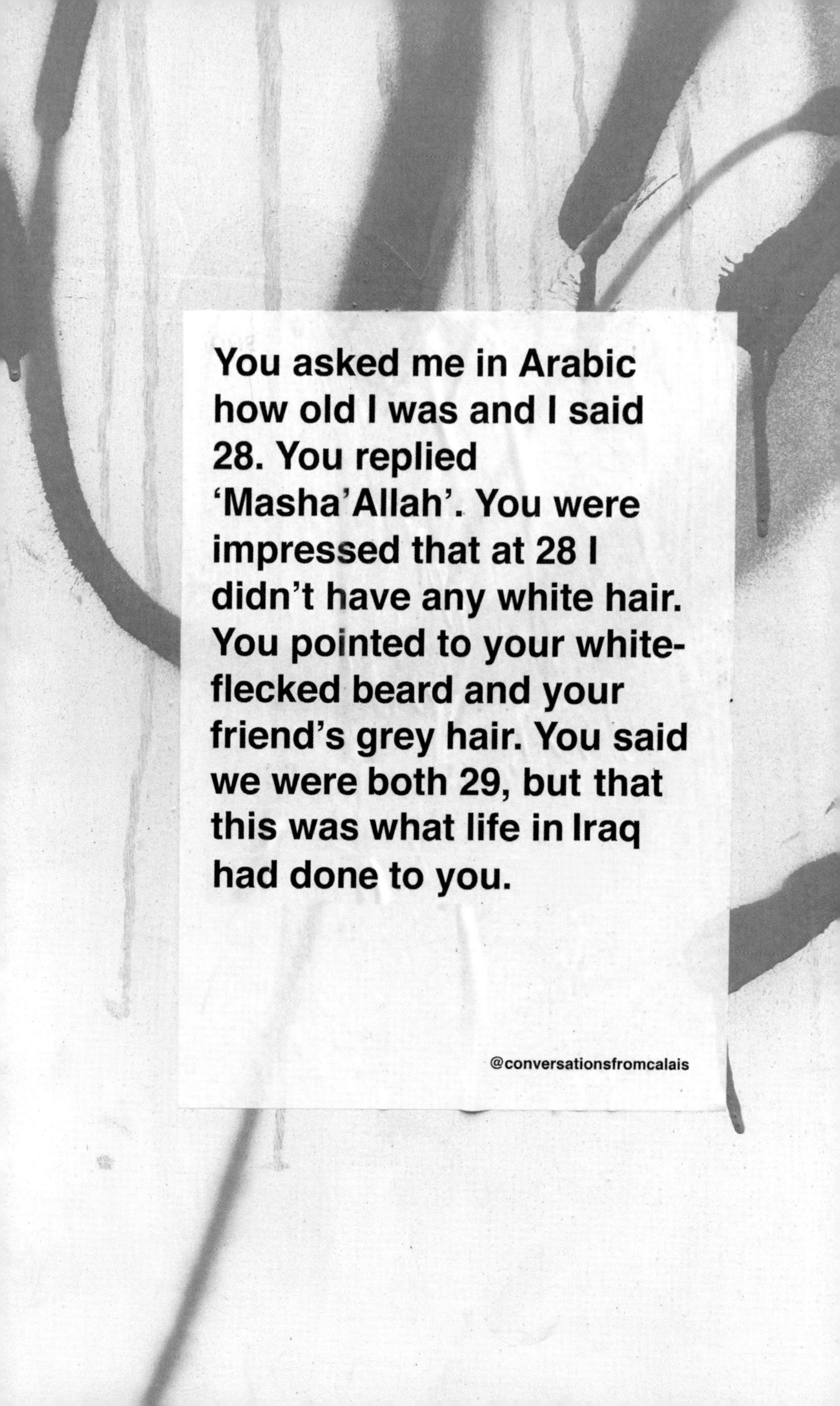

You asked me in Arabic how old I was and I said 28. You replied 'Masha'Allah'. You were impressed that at 28 I didn't have any white hair. You pointed to your white-flecked beard and your friend's grey hair. You said we were both 29, but that this was what life in Iraq had done to you.

@conversationsfromcalais

Four years later the Ugandan Asian crisis was set off by Idi Amin. The number on my passport back then was D 86092. That "D" was a mark of inferiority. I was "subject to control under the Commonwealth Immigrants Act"; white folk from Rhodesia, South Africa and elsewhere were not.

The number on my passport back then was D 86092. That "D" was a mark of inferiority. I was "subject to control under the Commonwealth Immigrants Act".

In 1971, the British, with their allies the US and Israel, backed a military coup against Milton Obote, the first elected socialist Ugandan leader. The West believed he would do their bidding. Within a year he expelled Asians. Far more serious, and crueller, were his crimes against black Ugandans – hundreds of thousands were killed, tortured or went into hiding.
We made new lives in Western countries and thrived; black Ugandans have had it much harder.

My dearest black Ugandan friend Sophie, who died two years ago in London, said this the last time we met: "I love you but cannot trust your people. They are still racist. We are both living in a safe country now. But I struggle every day and you don't." Asian and black Ugandans remain divided. Too many Britons still despise migrants. Ostensibly, Uganda and Britain are now open and global nations. But beneath the surface, old conflicts rage on.

YASMIN ALIBHAI-BROWN writes weekly columns for the *i* newspaper and features for other papers. She has written for the *Guardian*, the *Daily Mail*, *The Sunday Times*, the *New York Times*, *Time* magazine and other publications. She also broadcasts and makes radio programmes. Among her most recent books are *Ladies Who Punch*, *Exotic England*, *Refusing the Veil* and *In Defence of Political Correctness*. Her memoir, *The Settler's Cookbook*, on migration, love and food has just been reprinted. Some of this essay is taken from that book.

alibhai-brown.com
@y_alibhai

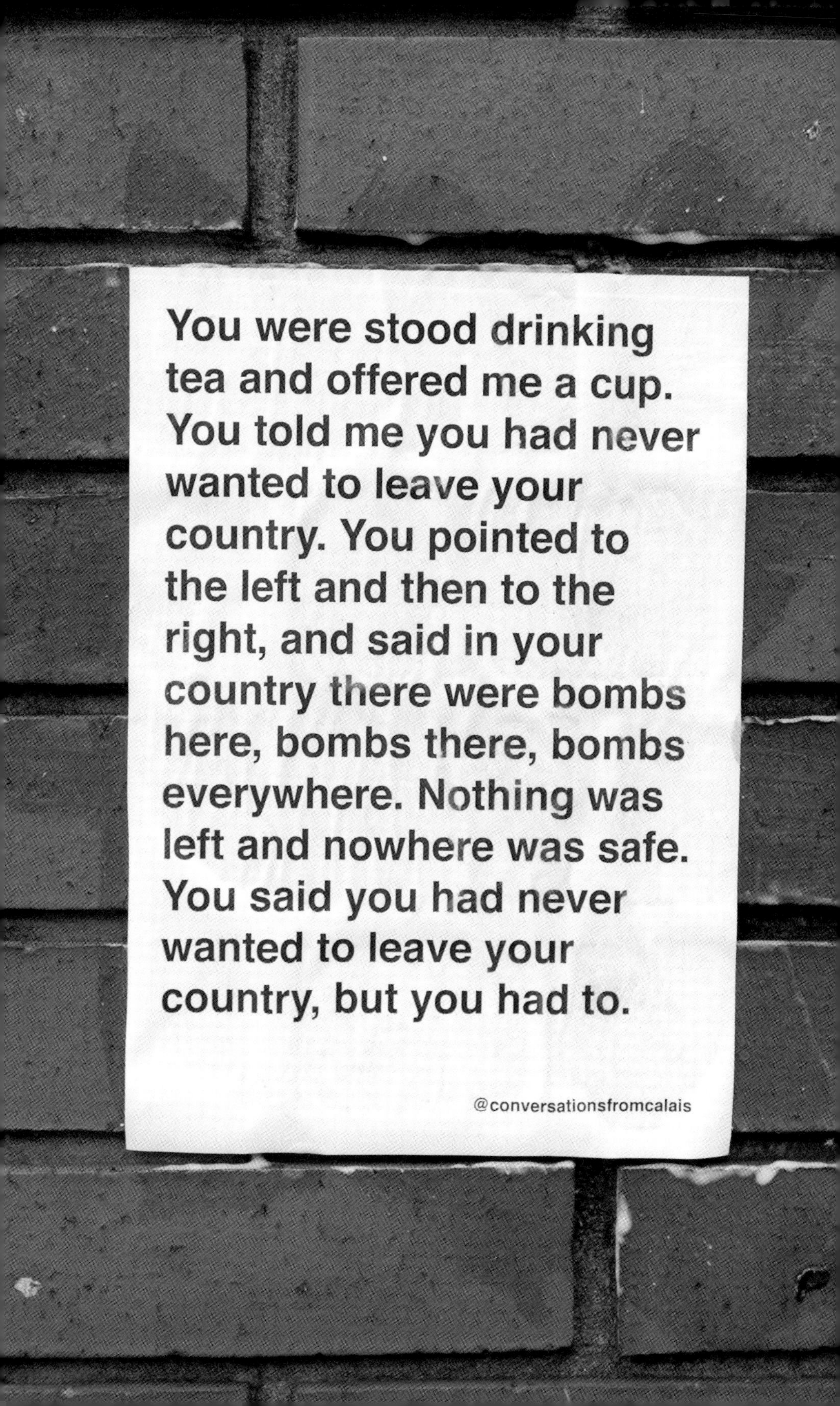

You were stood drinking tea and offered me a cup. You told me you had never wanted to leave your country. You pointed to the left and then to the right, and said in your country there were bombs here, bombs there, bombs everywhere. Nothing was left and nowhere was safe. You said you had never wanted to leave your country, but you had to.

@conversationsfromcalais

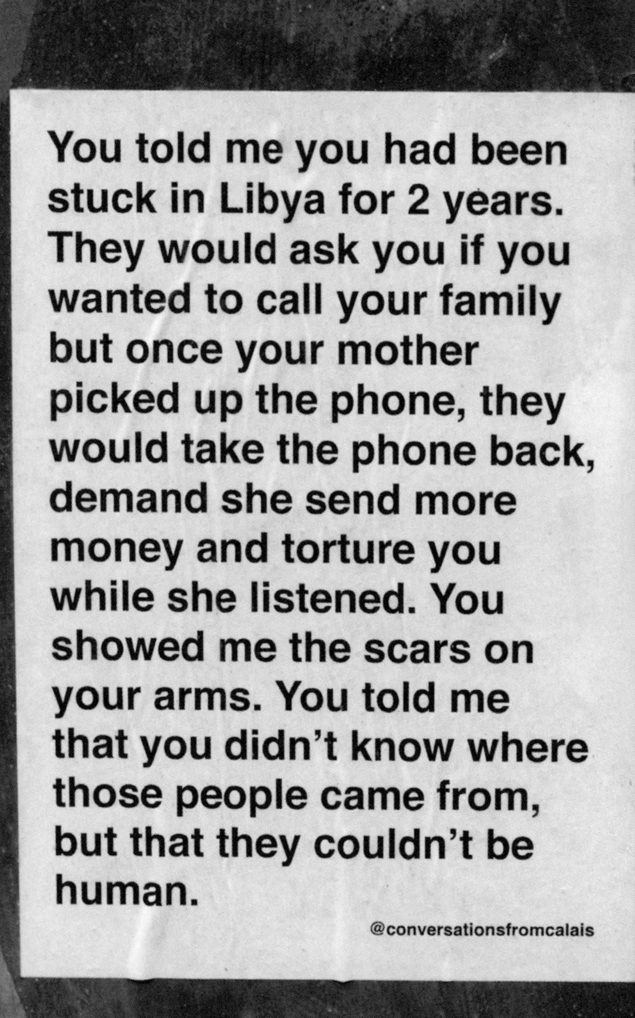
You told me you had been stuck in Libya for 2 years. They would ask you if you wanted to call your family but once your mother picked up the phone, they would take the phone back, demand she send more money and torture you while she listened. You showed me the scars on your arms. You told me that you didn't know where those people came from, but that they couldn't be human.
@conversationsfromcalais

plastic
ou
ecause
n
you
since
a year
ed
and
to
try
ber.
ved in
round
rney
ugee.

sfromcalais

You asked me if the world knew this was happening, if the world knew you were here, if the world knew your tent was taken from you almost every night, if the world knew the police was spraying tear gas on you almost every day, if the world knew this was living hell. And all I could do was whisper yes, yes the world knows.

@conversationsfromcalais

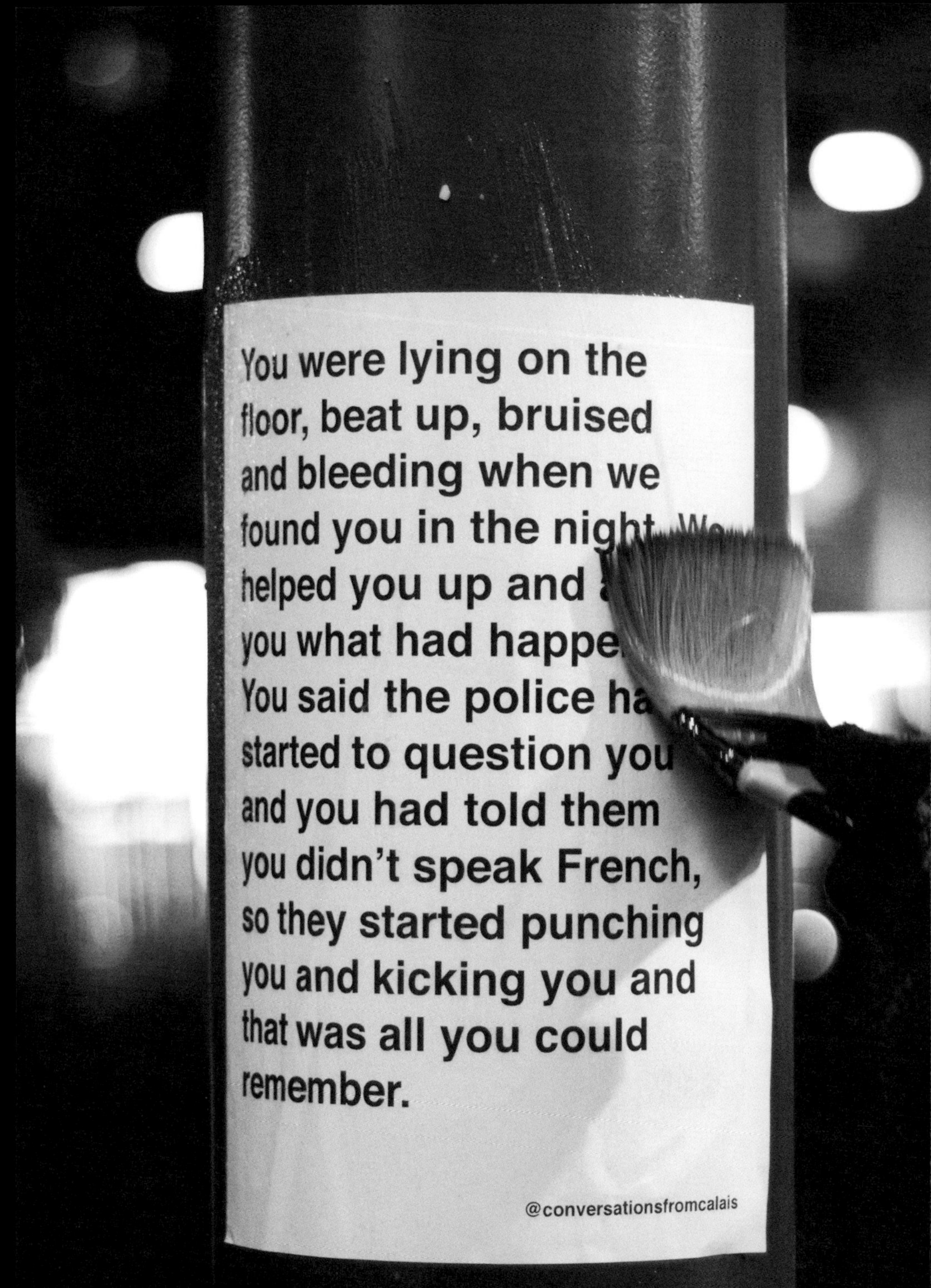

You were lying on the
floor, beat up, bruised
and bleeding when we
found you in the nig
helped you up and
you what had happe
You said the police ha
started to question you
and you had told them
you didn't speak French,
so they started punching
you and kicking you and
that was all you could
remember.

@conversationsfromcalais

You would always walk past me and say hi, with a tired look on your face. Today, during another eviction, you stood next to me in silence and watched as the police took all your belongings. Then you turned to me and said that you'd come here to flee Afghanistan, but that the police were the same here. The only difference was that they didn't have beards.

@conversationsfromcalais

“All too often when we discuss refugees we miss the most important voices of all, those of the refugees.”

DANIEL SOHEGE, Immigration lawyer & director of Stand For All

You were wearing flip flops
and it was 5°C out. I asked
you why and you a[illegible]wered
that the Fre[illegible]e had
chased you [illegible]ur
tent so violentl[illegible]ou
hadn't had time to [illegible]ur
boots on. You just ha[illegible]
run. Your tent and all you[illegible]
belongings had now been
burnt by the French police.
I knew the next distribution
of clothing wasn't for
another five days.

@conversationsfromcalais

You were telling me about how you tried last night. You pointed to a 3 year old girl and told me she was with you, in a bag, in the back of a lorry. When the police came to search the lorry, a police officer stood on the bag with her inside, but she didn't cry, she didn't make a sound, she knew she couldn't.

@conversationsfromcalais

You said your captors' faces haunted you at night. You couldn't stop thinking of them.

@conversationsfromcalais

07

FREEDOM & CHOICE

You wanted to play
football so we walked to
the grass and made two
teams. As always
team won. I said it
unfair because you
too good at running
the ball. You said it

ESSAY BY

AI WEIWEI

ARTIST

You told me your asylum claim had been rejected in Germany. The officer said you spoke such good English that you should try to go to England, even though you had learnt German. You told me that the promises of the EU were a lie, that every country just saw refugees as a problem to be sorted out by another country.

@conversationsfromcalais

FREE FROM FREEDOM

Making choices is difficult, not just for those who suffer from cross-border constraints, poverty, discrimination, and political and economic repression at an unimaginable level.

"Conversations" can be seen as our desire to communicate and understand on a spiritual and emotional level, often offering a chance for an awakening through a change of perspective. These different perspectives – although sometimes divisive – are the initiating condition for freedom. Our individual freedom is, in fact, the basis of conversation.

Freedom is about liberating ourselves from the constraints and boundaries imposed by politics, economics, culture and our own limited understanding of freedom. It is guided by "subject consciousness", which recognizes someone's unique personal experiences outside of the collective.

In Mandarin, the term for "freedom" – "自由自在" (pronunciation: zi you zi zai) – exemplifies how the existence of the subject (the individual) is key to the concept of freedom. Stemming from a Buddhist concept, the first two characters "自由" mean freedom, followed by "自在", which conveys the subject's state of ease. It is only when a person (the subject) has an awareness and an understanding of their individual consciousness that this state of ease emerges, bringing a rather harmonious relationship with one's own existence.

All our discourses, expression, creativity and deeds, out of existential needs only, reconfirm the definition of the state of ease.

Without being at ease with ourselves, it would be impossible to understand the scope of freedom and the desire to rid oneself of constraints. Yet it is important to remember that this state of ease, of freedom from within, does not necessarily have to depend on the outward conditions we experience. We do not have to free ourselves from all constraints to discover our individual consciousness.

"Conversations" can be seen as our desire to communicate and understand on a spiritual and emotional level, often offering a chance for an awakening through a change of perspective.

The concept of freedom nowadays is often viewed as something enjoyed by pleasure-seekers and the wealthy. It seems unattainable to those who will never be able to escape their plight. Freedom, however, is imperishable, like the stars in the sky. From cradle to grave, we all have aspirations and regrets. Freedom encompasses all of these. Making choices is difficult, not just for those who suffer from cross-border constraints, poverty, discrimination, and political and economic repression at an unimaginable level. Making choices flows from our own sense of self, and from challenging our awareness, ethics and moral judgement.

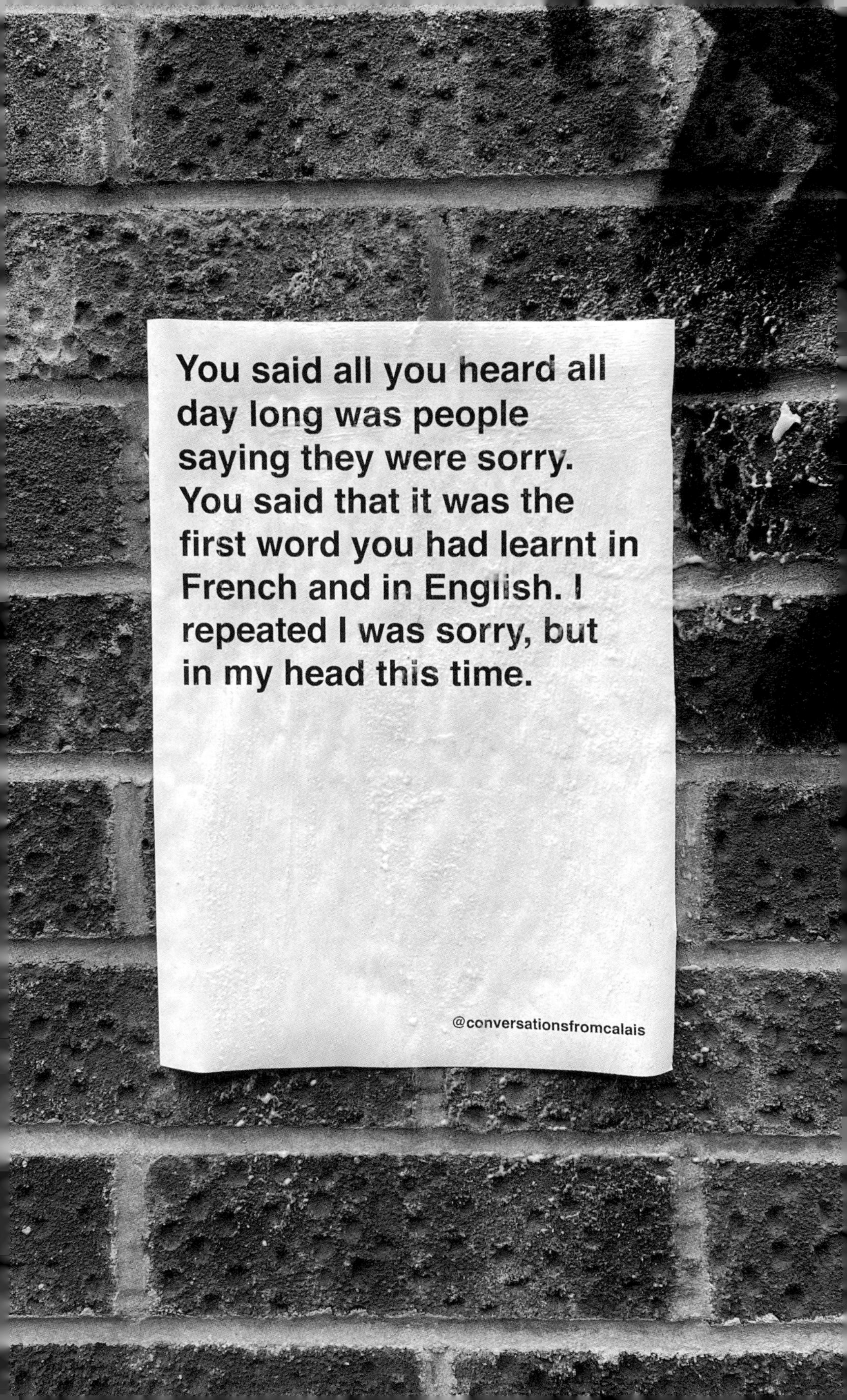
You said all you heard all day long was people saying they were sorry. You said that it was the first word you had learnt in French and in English. I repeated I was sorry, but in my head this time.
@conversationsfromcalais

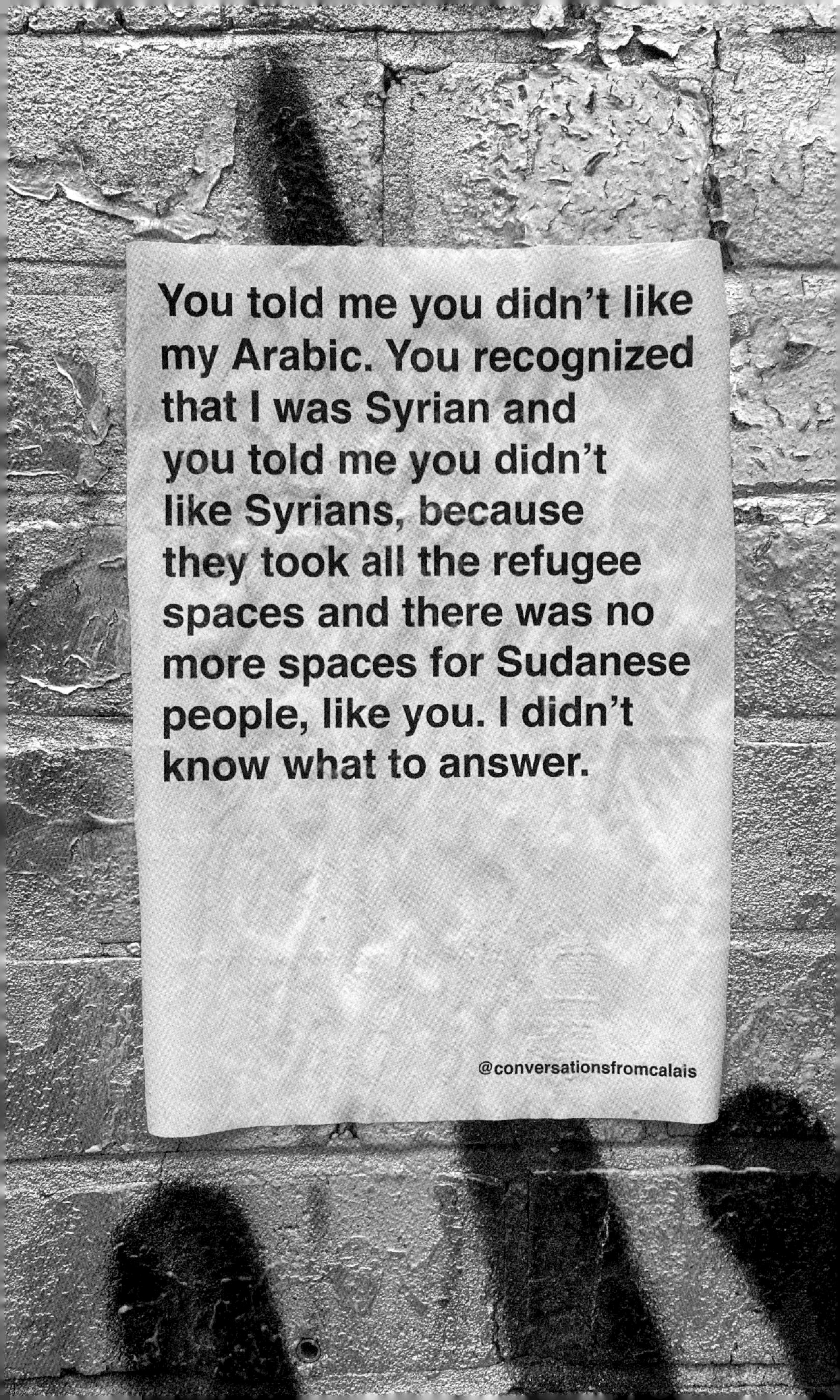
You told me you didn't like my Arabic. You recognized that I was Syrian and you told me you didn't like Syrians, because they took all the refugee spaces and there was no more spaces for Sudanese people, like you. I didn't know what to answer.
@conversationsfromcalais

When there is a risk to life because someone's basic human rights aren't being met, this often results in a yearning for civilization and community, over promoting our individualism. The choices we make, we make for the whole of society.
Our understanding of the link between humanitarianism and individual freedom will determine whether we remain dynamic or stagnate, and whether we choose to go forward or backward.

AI WEIWEI leads a diverse and prolific practice that encompasses sculptural installation, film-making, photography, ceramics, painting, writing and social media. A conceptual artist who fuses traditional craftsmanship and his Chinese heritage, Ai Weiwei moves freely between a variety of formal languages to reflect on the contemporary geopolitical and sociopolitical condition. Ai Weiwei's work and life regularly interact and inform one another, often extending to his activism and advocacy for international human rights.

aiweiwei.com
@aiww

You came over looking the happiest I had ever seen you. I asked you how you were doing and you said good, because you felt like tonight was going to be the night. It was going to be the night when all this was worth it. The night when you would run and you would get on a lorry and the police wouldn't see you and you would make it to the UK.
You asked me if the world knew this was happening, if the world knew you were here, if the world knew your tent was taken from you almost every night, if the world knew the police was spraying tear gas on you almost every day, if the world knew this was living hell. And all I could do was whisper yes, yes the world knows.
You wanted to play football so we walked to the grass and made two teams. As always your team won. I said it was unfair because you were too good at running away with the ball. You said it was unfair because I could run away anywhere in the world and no one would stop me.
You showed me a picture of your family you treasured in your pocket. You said you kept in touch with them, but lied to them about this situation. You told them you were staying in a hotel, not in a tent, because you didn't want them to worry and because this way you could hold on to another reality.
You asked me if I could get you a paper, a pen and a flashlight. I said I could try and asked why you needed these things. You said because you were going to write a book about how it was like being a refugee in Europe. You said you would write it here in Calais and then publish it when you made it to the UK. I said I couldn't wait to read it.
You were helping me pick up the trash around the camp, when you saw the police drive by and said the police was no good. I replied that you were right, that the police was not protecting you, that the police was no good. You were only nine years old.
You didn't want a green or purple sweater, you wanted a black one. We didn't have any black ones left so I offered you a dark blue one. You looked at me and asked if one day you'd have a choice again. I told you I really hoped so and handed you the dark blue sweater.
You were sat in a field full of tents and people under the cold sun. You were by yourself, looking at the ground, silently crying. I approached you and asked you if I could help or if I could get you anything. Through your tears you said you just wanted a passport. You were 10 years old.
You told me in Iran the pomegranates were sweeter and the flowers brighter. You drew a rose and wrote it in Farsi, so I taught you how to say the colours in French. You said drawing was easier and that it helped you remember. I said it helped me not to forget. You said red was your favourite colour, but that Iran had lost all its colour.
You asked me how I was doing and I said I didn't want to go back to the UK tomorrow but that I had to. You laughed at me and said that we lived in a strange world, because reaching the UK was all you had ever wanted.
You wanted a new toothbrush and a boat to cross the sea. I gave you the toothbrush and apologised about not having a boat. You said your bag was heavy, your legs tired and your hands cold. I gave you a cup of tea and apologised about the cold. You added sugar and walked away.
You had taught yourself how to speak nine new languages from the day you left your home, so you could speak with the people of every country you crossed. I said I didn't know anyone who could speak this many languages. You replied that it was useless anyway, because no one ever wanted to speak to you, let alone look at you.

ere an
been
now
you
ause
your
ou
ildren
get

sfromcalais

You looked up and said the sky was beautiful today. I replied that yes, it was. In that moment, we were just two people looking up at the sky.

@conversationsfromcalais

You were no older than sixteen. Having to wait in line for food and second hand clothes was unthinkable. You said nothing was more important to you than your honour and your dignity. You said that you had been tortured in Libya, but that your dignity was untouched. But Calais was ripping your dignity out of your chest.

@conversationsfromcalais

“These stories shared humanise those who are too often dehumanised by the media and politicians. I am forced to stop in my tracks when reading a ‘conversation’. They have moved people to act, volunteer, to protest, to care about our fellow human beings.”

MIKAELA LOACH, Climate justice activist

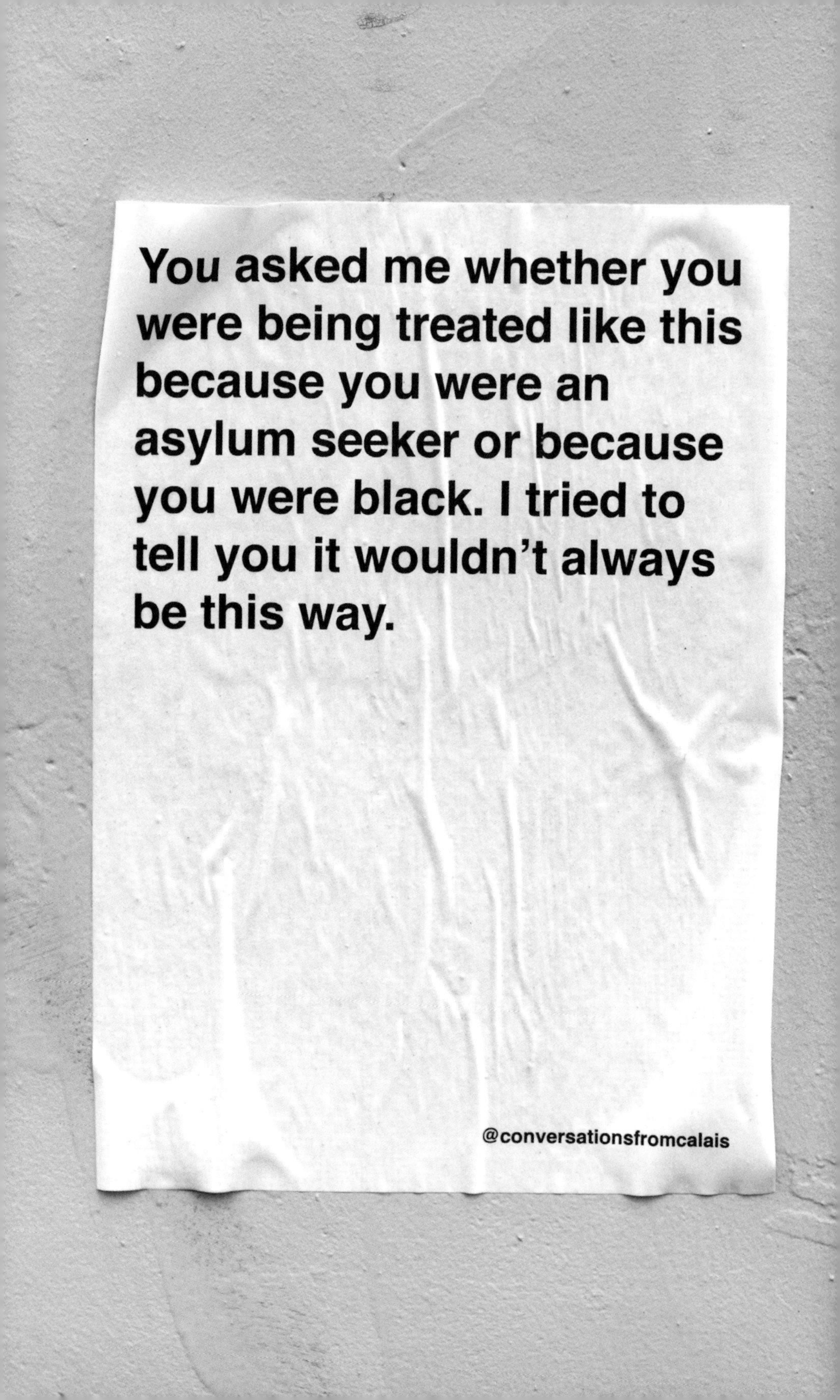

You asked me whether you were being treated like this because you were an asylum seeker or because you were black. I tried to tell you it wouldn't always be this way.

@conversationsfromcalais

You told me everyone left Afghanistan. Americans, Italians, French, British, everyone. You asked me why did you have to stay there then.

@conversationsfromcalais

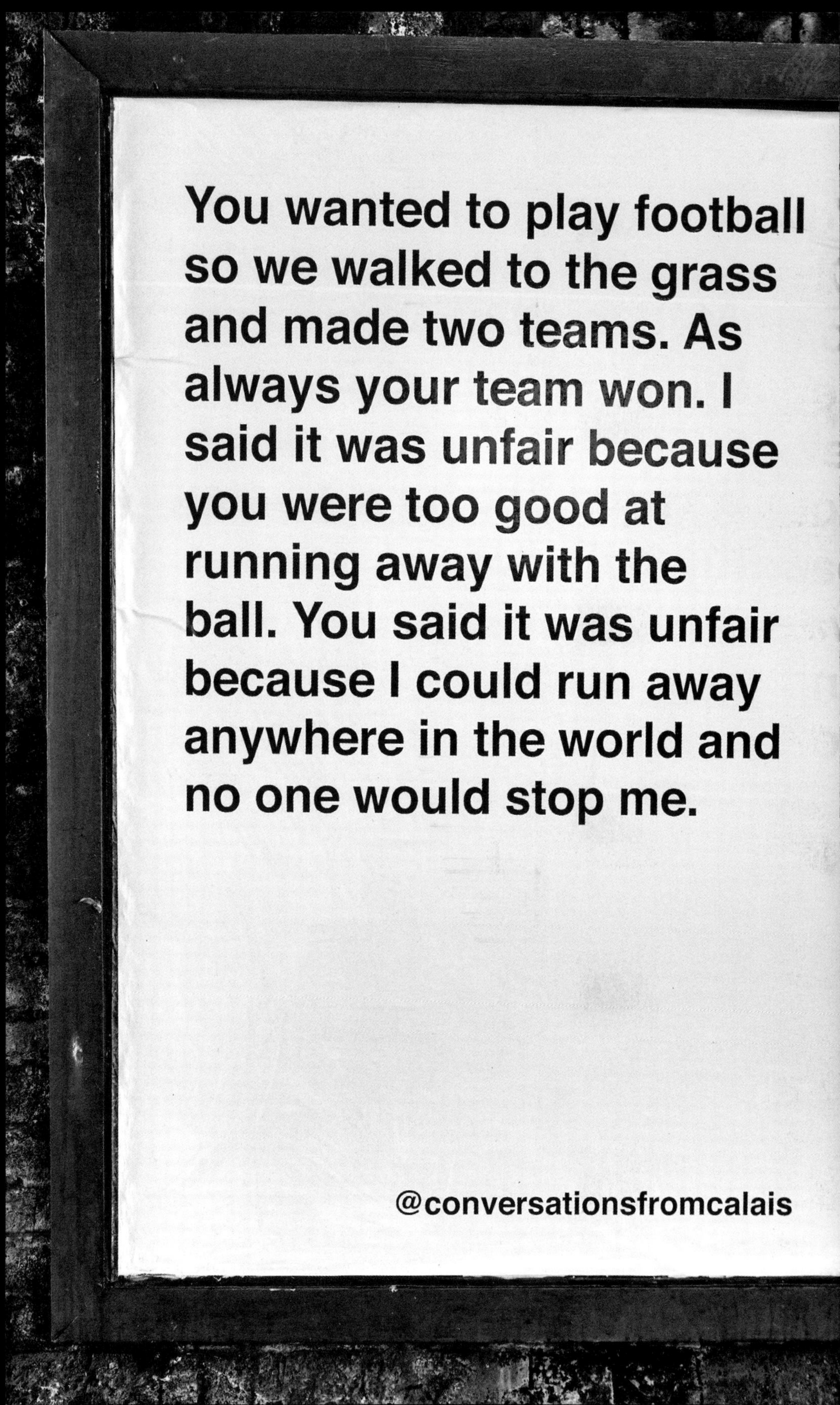

You wanted to play football so we walked to the grass and made two teams. As always your team won. I said it was unfair because you were too good at running away with the ball. You said it was unfair because I could run away anywhere in the world and no one would stop me.

@conversationsfromcalais

ou told

lympian

Rio in

ou were

elt suffo

ou could

assion.

anted to

nd could

our pape

You didn't want a green or purple sweater, you wanted a black one. We didn't have any black ones left so I offered you a dark blue one. You looked at me and asked if one day you'd have a choice again. I told you I really hoped so and handed you the dark blue sweater.

@conversationsfromcalais

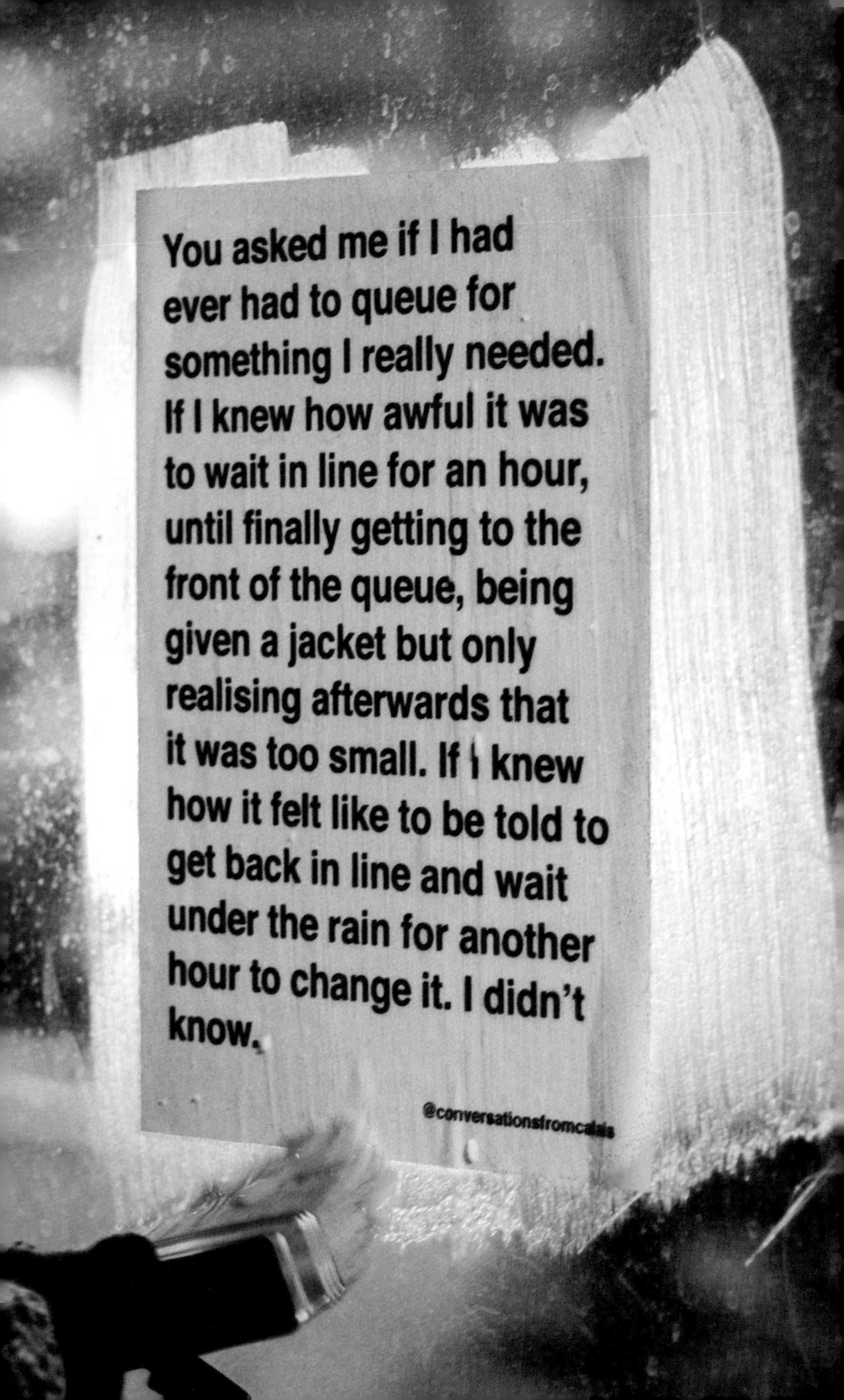

You asked me if I had ever had to queue for something I really needed. If I knew how awful it was to wait in line for an hour, until finally getting to the front of the queue, being given a jacket but only realising afterwards that it was too small. If I knew how it felt like to be told to get back in line and wait under the rain for another hour to change it. I didn't know.

@conversationsfromcalais

You watched me as I made mayonnaise sandwiches and wrapped them in sheets of newspaper. You pointed at the English flag on one of the sheets and said you liked that flag. I smiled and thought to myself how much life made fun of us: your dream, right there, under a mayonnaise sandwich.

@conversationsfromcalais

08

HOPE & FUTURE

You had studied the same
thing as me. We'd
our engineering
the same age. We
about the classes we
the homework we both
hated, the teachers that
made it all worthwhile. You
said you wanted to design
bridges when you got to
the UK.

ESSAY BY

INUA ELLAMS

POET, PLAYWRIGHT & PERFORMER

You told me you were an Olympian who had been to Rio in 2016, but now you were here and you felt suffocated because you couldn't follow your passion. You said you wanted to coach children and couldn't wait to get your papers.

@conversationsfromcalais

BLUE SKIES & DARK WATERS

There's a photo on my phone of three men in deepest open water. Though its surface is blue, and as such holds the promise of the sky and the freedom the sky has always suggested, there is darkness beneath.

In the far distance, in the top right corner of the photo, you can see the great hulking mass of a shipping dock, where a metal crane scuffs the clear blue of the skyline. There's also a metal ship, wide and grey, long and rusty – a fortress of a thing – a mechanical beast of the sea.

How desperate must one be to take such a risk and such a journey.

That ship gives an idea, perhaps, of the scale of what it is the three men are perched on, because we can't see. We can't tell for sure. They are in the centre of the photograph, in its foreground, and the three men are sat on a ship's rudder. I know it is a rudder because the caption beneath the photo tells me so. A rudder is the primary control surface used to steer a ship, and this rudder is long enough to hold three men, which suggests how large a ship it is attached to.

The ship is mostly painted red. The red paint is peeling, exposing patches of metal. These metal patches, now exposed to air, are dark with rust, and among all the red and rust, the metal and decay, this conglomerate of money and machine, are the three men. They are hunched over, sat on the rudder, because there isn't room enough to stand or stretch.

They are hunched over, with their necks so bent that their chins are resting on their chests, and the caption beneath the photo reads: "Three men found on ship's rudder after 11-day voyage". I become aware of my own neck, how I am bending down to look at this photo on my phone. I have been holding this position for a handful of seconds, and the strain on the back of my neck is already unbearable. But I choose to keep my neck there, as if to honour these men, who held a similar position – their chins touching their chests – for 11 whole days.

The caption carries on: "The ship had arrived in Las Palmas, Gran Canaria, from Nigeria's largest city, Lagos – a journey of over 2,700 nautical miles ... A photo shared by the Spanish coastguards shows their feet less than a metre above the water, as they sit on the rudder at the oil tanker's stern." And several thoughts occur to me ...

1. The story of oil and Nigeria is the story of violence and exploitation.
2. The story of violence and exploitation is the story of displacement and migration.
3. The story of displacement and migration is the story of blood and water.
4. The story of blood and water is also the story of hope and the future.
5. The story of hope and the future is every immigrant's story.

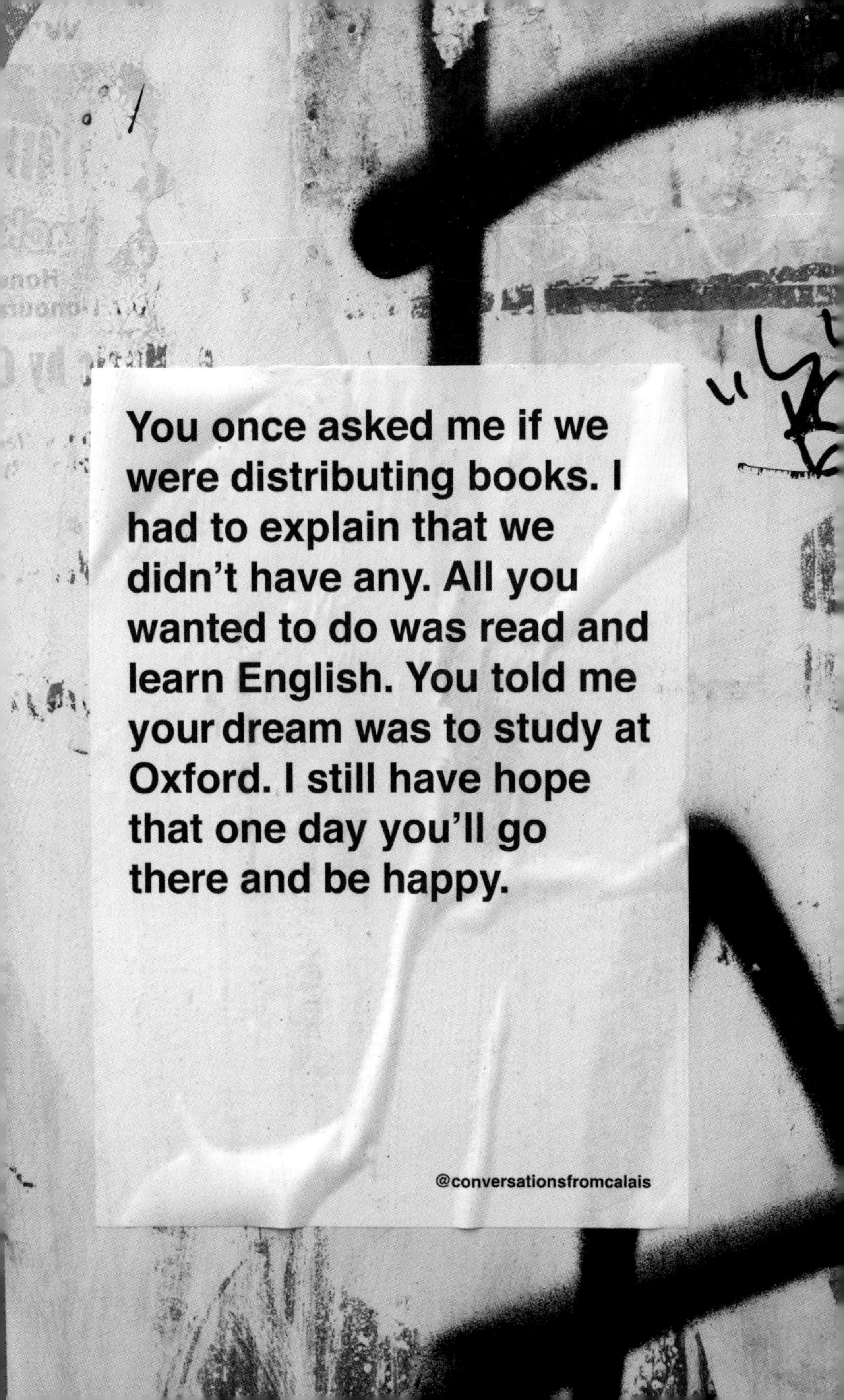
You once asked me if we were distributing books. I had to explain that we didn't have any. All you wanted to do was read and learn English. You told me your dream was to study at Oxford. I still have hope that one day you'll go there and be happy.
@conversationsfromcalais

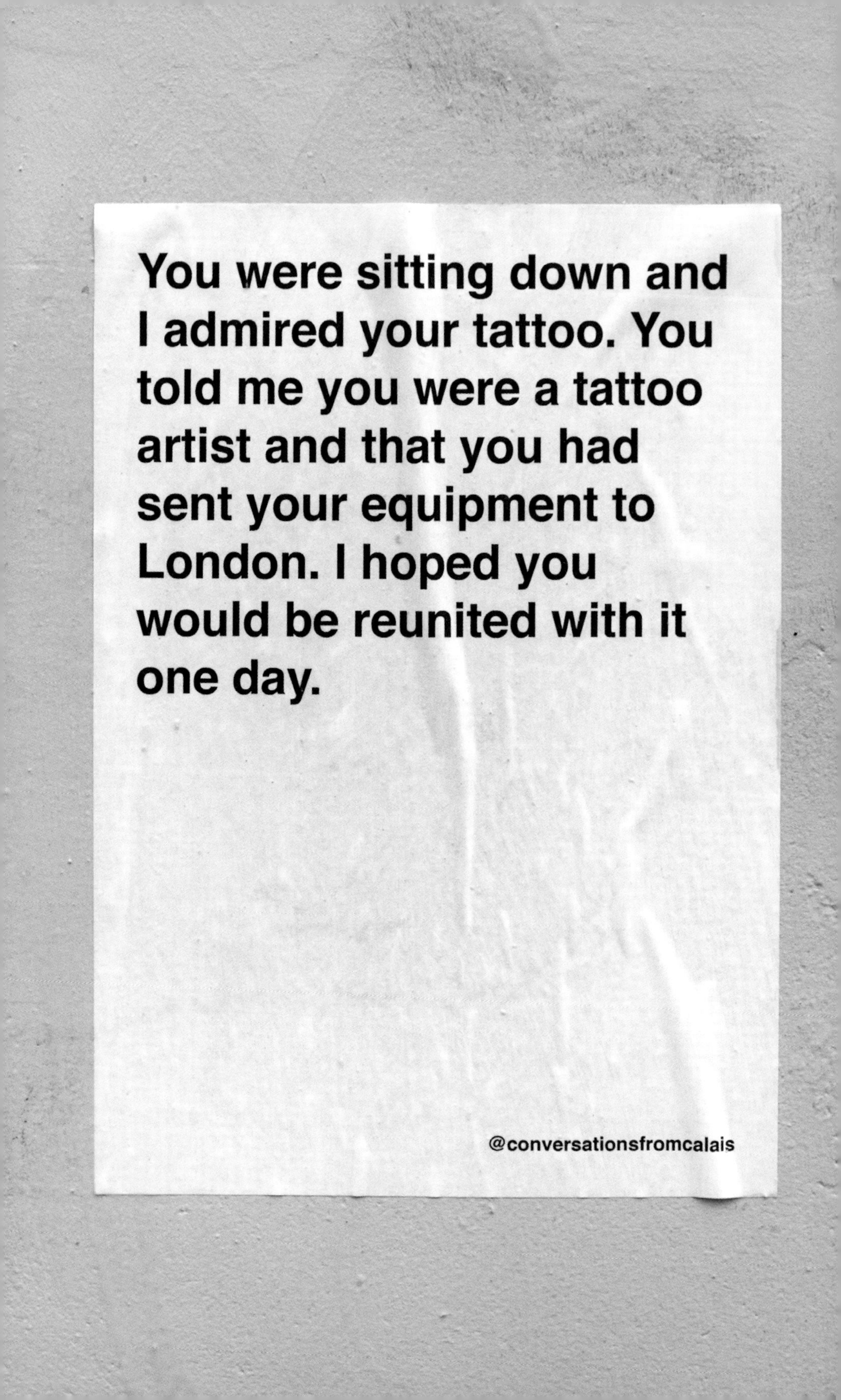

You were sitting down and I admired your tattoo. You told me you were a tattoo artist and that you had sent your equipment to London. I hoped you would be reunited with it one day.

@conversationsfromcalais

This photo on my phone tells this story. It is the world on their shoulders, the empire kneeling on their necks, their faces bent towards darkness, 11 days sailing over certain death, and the hope that clinging on will deliver a better future.

Usually, photos like this are followed by horrendous comments. They typically read:

"Europe is full"
"We have to keep them out"
"Send them back"
"Deport them now"
"We need a final solution"

There *are* such comments, but they are few and far between, and overwhelmed by comments like these:

"How desperate must one be to take such a risk and such a journey"
"We really do need a better world"
"They risked everything for a better life"
"Please let them stay"

As a Nigerian, as an immigrant, there is much more I can say, but all I can hope is our future is the one in which they were allowed to stayed.

There's a photo on my phone of three men in deepest open water. Though its surface is blue, and as such holds the promise of the sky and the freedom the sky had always suggested, there is darkness beneath.

Born in Nigeria, **INUA ELLAMS** is an internationally touring poet, playwright, performer, graphic artist and designer. His published books of poetry include *Candy-Coated Unicorns and Converse All Stars*, *Thirteen Fairy Negro Tales*, *The Wire-Headed Heathen*, *#Afterhours*, *The Half-God of Rainfall* and *The Actual*. His first play, *The 14th Tale*, was awarded a Fringe First at the Edinburgh International Theatre Festival, and his fourth, *Barber Shop Chronicles* sold out two runs at England's National Theatre. In graphic art and design, online and in print, he tries to mix the old with the new, juxtaposing texture and pigment with flat colour and vector graphics.

inuaellams.com
@inuaellams

BUILDHOLLYWOOD
You sat down to charge your phone and when it turned on, you held it close to your chest, closed your eyes and smiled. You handed me your phone, so I could see the Facebook message from your brother who said he had made it to the UK last night and that he was safe. You looked at me and said this is why you were still here, still hoping.
@conversationsfromcalais
4014 03
BUILDHOLLYWOOD

Acton Works
130 Bollo Lane
Pedestrian entrance
Please report to Security

“These conversations lean into one of our earliest means of connection; the sharing of stories. Placing a spotlight on the humanity, similarity and normalness of those whose stories we are most in need of hearing, reminding us that the only difference between ourselves and anyone else is circumstance.”

OLIVE GRAY, Actor

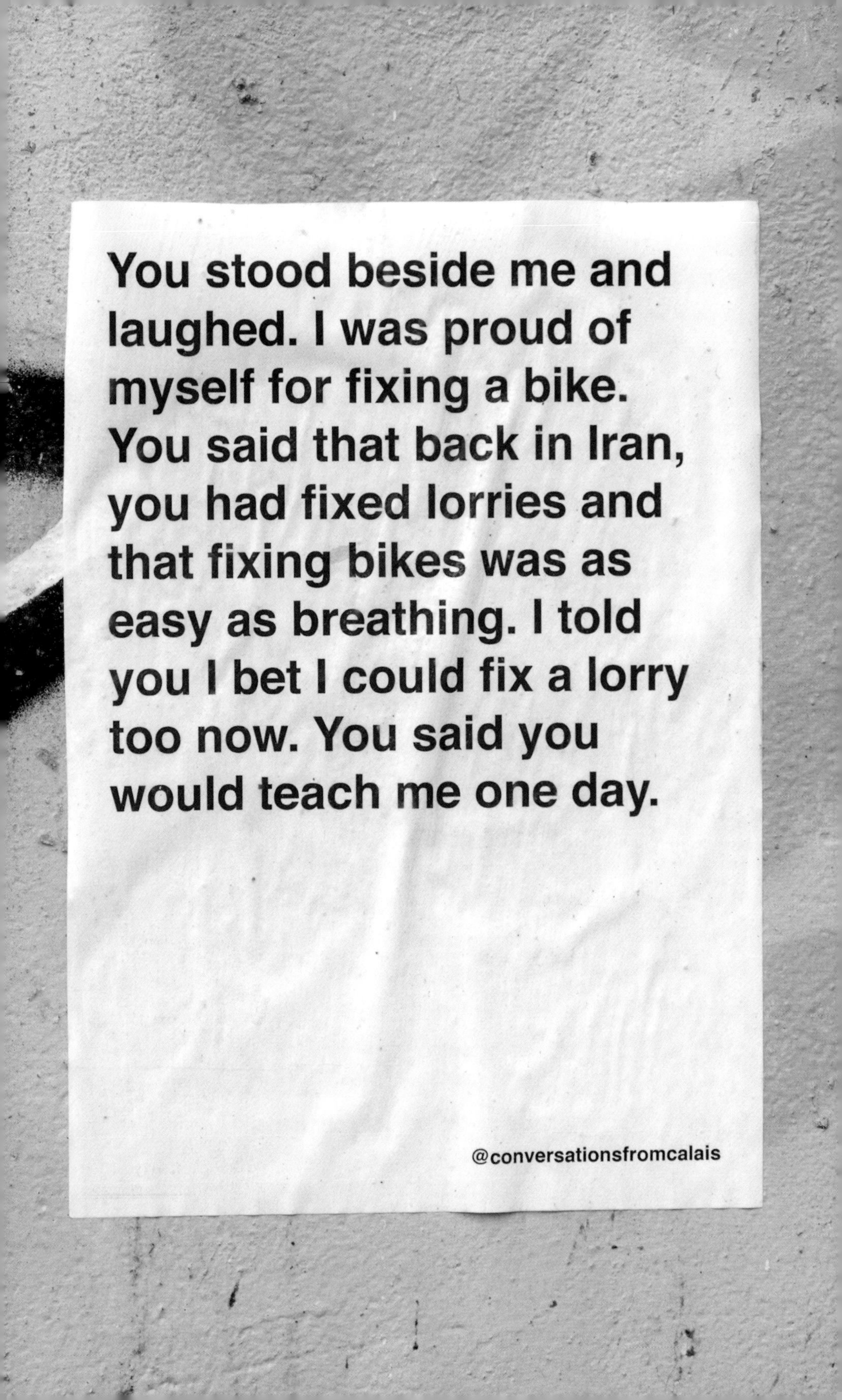

You stood beside me and laughed. I was proud of myself for fixing a bike. You said that back in Iran, you had fixed lorries and that fixing bikes was as easy as breathing. I told you I bet I could fix a lorry too now. You said you would teach me one day.

@conversationsfromcalais

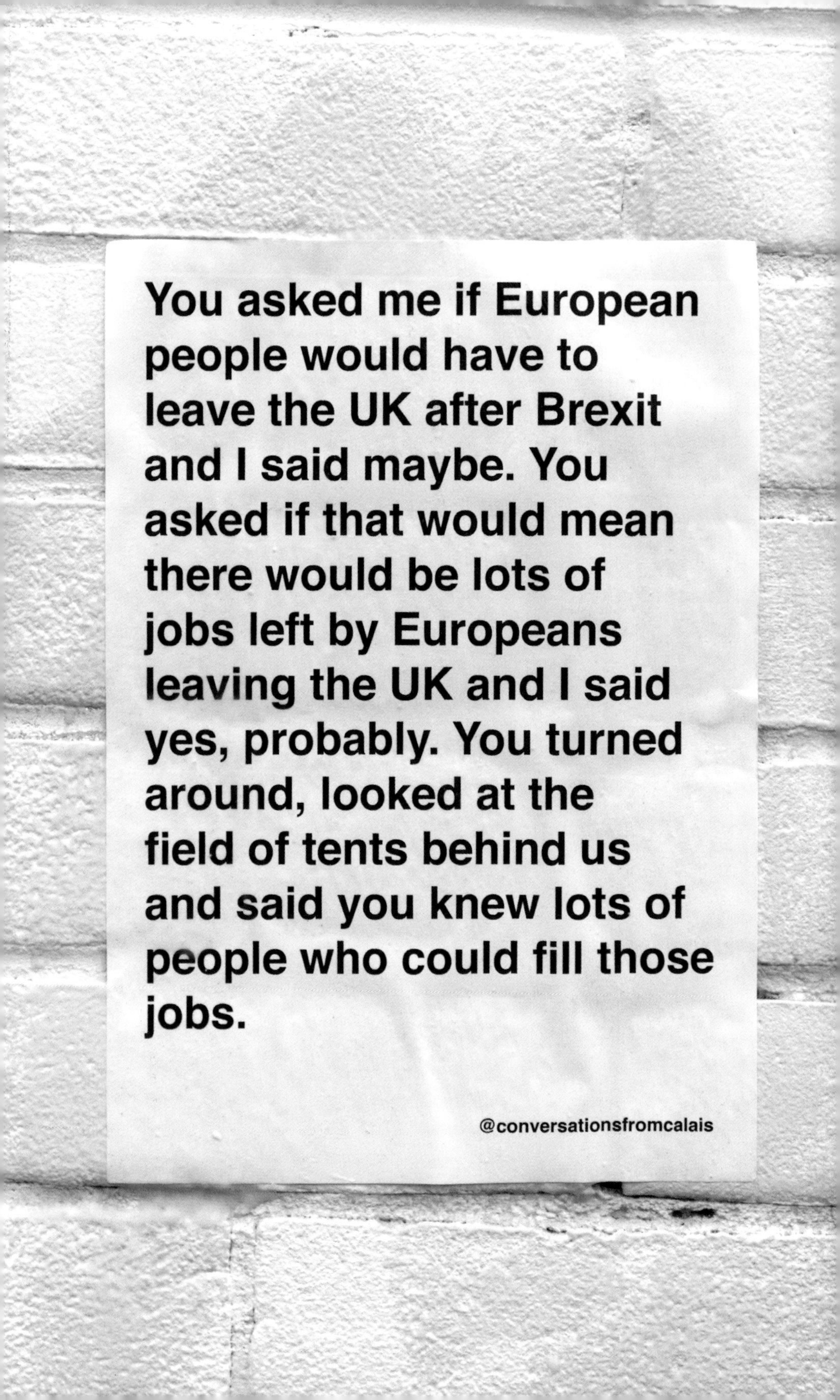

You asked me if European people would have to leave the UK after Brexit and I said maybe. You asked if that would mean there would be lots of jobs left by Europeans leaving the UK and I said yes, probably. You turned around, looked at the field of tents behind us and said you knew lots of people who could fill those jobs.

@conversationsfromcalais

You were talking to me about your past. I asked you what your goal in life was. You said you wanted to open free healthcare in every country so everyone could access it. You said that we should never put wealth over health.

You asked me if I co
get you a paper, a pe
a flashlight. I said I cou
try and asked why you
needed these things. You
said you were going to
write a book about how it
was like being a refugee
in Europe. You said you
would write it here in
then publish it
he
to

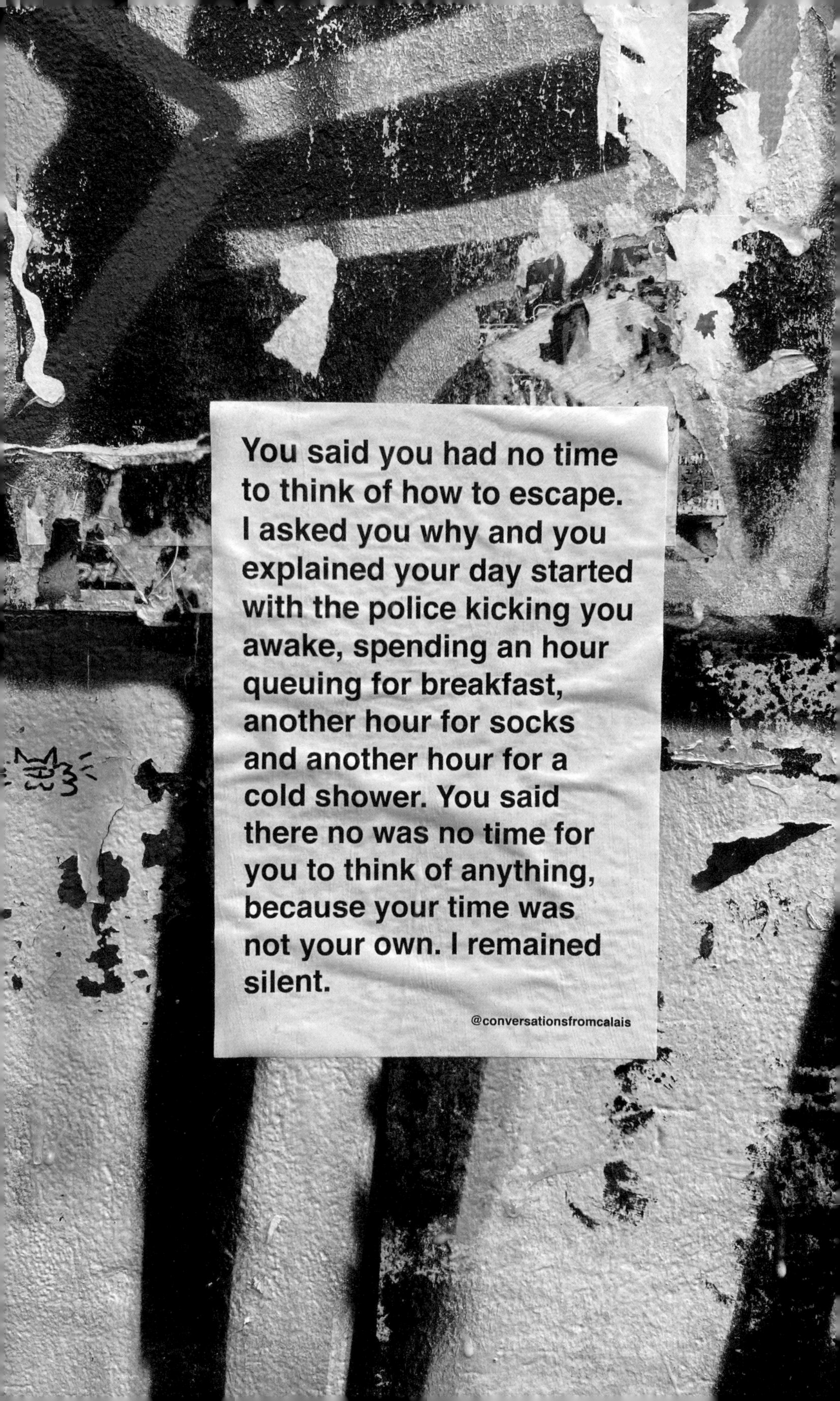
You said you had no time
to think of how to escape.
I asked you why and you
explained your day started
with the police kicking you
awake, spending an hour
queuing for breakfast,
another hour for socks
and another hour for a
cold shower. You said
there no was no time for
you to think of anything,
because your time was
not your own. I remained
silent.
@conversationsfromcalais

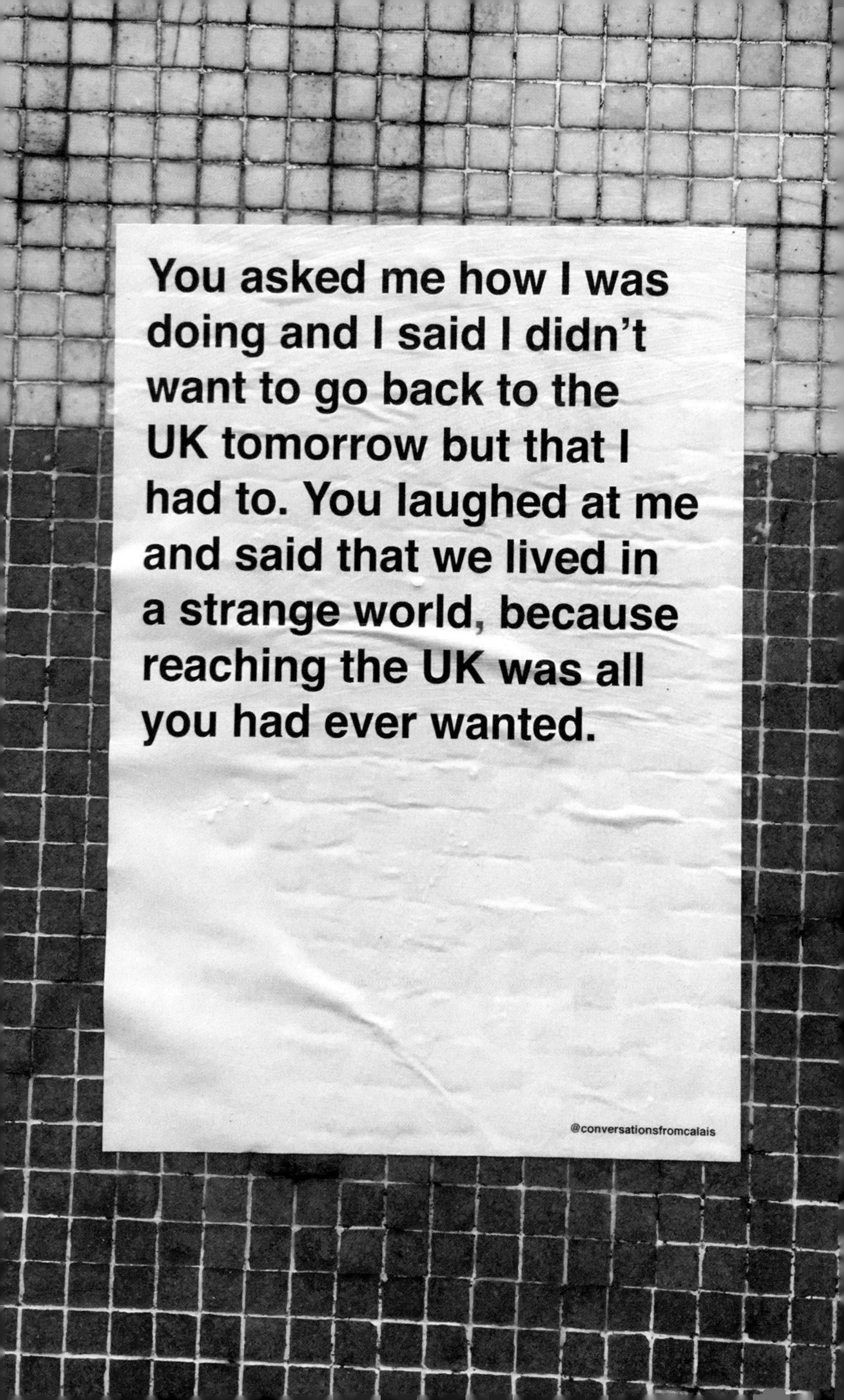

You asked me how I was doing and I said I didn't want to go back to the UK tomorrow but that I had to. You laughed at me and said that we lived in a strange world, because reaching the UK was all you had ever wanted.

@conversationsfromcalais

You said you wanted to write a book once you had claimed asylum. I asked if you had written notes. You said you didn't need any, as you would never forget the things you'd seen.

@conversationsfromcalais

ACKNOWLEDGEMENTS

First and foremost, thank you to all the displaced people I met in Calais for sharing your stories. I will carry our conversations with me forever and I hope this book does them justice.

Thank you to all the volunteers who, over the years, have taken the time to send me the conversations they've had. This project would be nowhere without you. Beth, Frankie, Maddy, Otis and Sophie – thank you for sharing your experiences.

Thank you, Emma, for seeing the importance of this work and for always standing beside me. Thank you, Jo, for your trust and your patience, I still can't believe we made this happen.

Thank you, Ai Weiwei, Gulwali Passarlay, Joudie Kalla, Inua Ellams, Nish Kumar, Osman Yousefzada, Waad Al-Kateab and Yasmin Alibhai-Brown – your stories complete this book, and I hope they inspire others as much as they inspire me.

Thank you, Daniel Sohege, Emma Gannon, Hassan Akkad, Jaz O'hara, Kamila Shamsie, Khaled Hosseini, Lord Alf Dubs, Magid Magid, Mark Titchner, Mikaela Loach, Olive Gray, Onjali Q Rauf, Rifaie Tammas and Stanislava Pinchuk – your words helped so much in bringing this book to life.

Thank you to all those who have contributed to this project in small or big ways by pasting posters somewhere in the world, sharing them on social media, translating them, or simply encouraging me to keep going – it really does take a village.

Thank you to all the grassroots organisations providing essential support and refusing to turn their backs on displaced communities in northern France.

Thank you to the entire Freedom From Torture team, whose work I will forever be grateful for. It's an honour to be able to use this book to support you in a small way.

Thank you, Omar, for always reminding me it would be worth it. Thank you to my Julies, my Doggos and all of my girls, for being my biggest cheerleaders and my sunshines. And finally, Mam, Papi and Teo – thank you for everything, always and forever.

FURTHER RESOURCES

Conversations From Calais should only be used as a starting point to delve deeper into refugee rights. I hope your next steps are to engage with work created by people with lived experienced and to support and mobilise with organisations in your local community.

Books

- *The Actual* by Inua Ellams. Penned in the Margins, 2020.
- *The Boy At The Back of the Class* by Onjali Q. Rauf. Orion Children's Books, 2018.
- *The Go-Between: A Portrait of Growing Up Between Different Worlds* by Osman Yousefzada. Canongate Books, 2022.
- *Border Nation: A Story of Migration* by Leah Cowan. Pluto Press, 2021.
- *The Displaced: Refugee Writers on Refugee Lives* by Viet Thanh Nguyen. Abrams Press, 2019.
- *Hostile Environment: How Immigrants Became Scapegoats* by Maya Goodfellow. Verso, 2020.
- *The Lightless Sky: My Journey to Safety as a Child Refugee* by Gulwali Passarlay. Atlantic Books, 2018.
- *The Ungrateful Refugee: What Immigrants Never Tell You* by Dina Nayeri. Canongate Books, 2020.

Documentaries

- *Flee* by Jonas Poher Rasmussen, 2022.
- *For Sama* by Waad al-Kateab, 2019.
- *Human Flow* by Ai Weiwei, 2017.
- *Midnight Traveler* by Hassan Fazili, 2019.

Podcast

- *Asylum Speakers Podcast with Jaz O'Hara: Stories of Migration*

Organisations to support

- *Art Refuge* use art and art therapy to support the mental health and wellbeing of people displaced in the UK and internationally – www.artrefuge.org.uk
- *Calais Appeal* is a group of eight grassroots organisations providing essential support to displaced people in Calais and Dunkirk – www.calaisappeal.co.uk
- *Freedom from Torture* supports people who have survived torture to heal, feel safe and strong again (see overleaf).
- *International Rescue Committee* respond to the world's worst humanitarian crises by helping people to survive, recover and rebuild their lives – www.rescue.org
- *Refugee Action* provide services, support and advice to refugees in the UK – www.refugee-action.org.uk
- *Safe Passage* help child refugees access their rights in the UK – www.safepassage.org.uk
- *UNHCR* is the United Nations Refugee Agency protecting refugees, forcibly displaced communities and stateless peoples worldwide – www.unhcr.org

FOR EVERY COPY OF THIS BOOK SOLD MATHILDA AND WELBECK PUBLISHING GROUP WILL MAKE A CHARITY DONATION TO FREEDOM FROM TORTURE

Freedom from Torture supports people who have survived torture to heal, feel safe and strong again.

Our vision is a world free from torture. We aim to ensure that the human rights of survivors are restored through rehabilitation and protection. We fight to ensure that states responsible for torture are held to account.

Our therapists work with survivors to rebuild their physical and mental health. Our doctors document evidence of torture, and our lawyers and welfare advisors help survivors with their asylum cases and social support. We also support other organisations delivering high-quality rehabilitation services. Together, we speak out to expose torture and defend the rights of survivors, nationally and globally. We hold torturing governments to account. And we campaign for women, men and children to be treated fairly when they seek safety in the UK after being tortured.